THE TALLEY METHOD

Plays by S. N. Behrman

THE SECOND MAN

METEOR

SERENA BLANDISH

BRIEF MOMENT

BIOGRAPHY

RAIN FROM HEAVEN

END OF SUMMER

AMPHITRYON 38
Adapted from the French of Jean Giraudoux

WINE OF CHOICE

NO TIME FOR COMEDY

S · N · BEHRMAN

THE TALLEY METHOD

A PLAY IN THREE ACTS

R H

RANDOM HOUSE · NEW YORK

First Printing

MANUFACTURED IN THE UNITED STATES OF AMERICA

For Robert Emmet Sherwood

The Talley Method was produced by The Playwrights' Company at Henry Miller's Theatre on February 24, 1941, with the following cast:

(*In the order in which they speak*)

AVIS TALLEY	Claire Niesen
PHILIP TALLEY	Dean Harens
CY BLODGETT	Hiram Sherman
ENID FULLER	Ina Claire
MARY	Lida Kane
MANFRED GEIST	Ernst Deutsch
DR. AXTON TALLEY	Philip Merivale

Settings by JO MIELZINER

Modern Drama Class
Dept of Speech
1941

SCENE

The play takes place in the upstairs living room of Dr. Talley's office residence in an old brownstone house in the East Sixties in New York City. The time is the present—late spring.

ACT ONE

Late afternoon.

ACT TWO

Late afternoon. A few days later.

ACT THREE

Late evening of the same day.

ACT ONE

ACT ONE

The scene is the upstairs living room at Dr. Talley's in an old brownstone house in the East Sixties in New York City. The house is a combination office and residence. The furniture is a mixture of antique and modern. Somehow, though, the amalgam is homely and cheerful rather than grotesque. Tea time of an afternoon in early Spring.

AVIS *and* PHILIP TALLEY *are on stage when curtain goes up.* PHILIP *is twenty-one, anxious, sensitive and charming-looking.* AVIS *is brilliantly attractive, a year or so younger.* PHILIP *sits on chair center, one leg over arm of chair, reading a book of verse.* AVIS *is at the telephone. She holds the receiver to her ear.*

AVIS

(*Hanging up*)

Still busy!

PHILIP

Are you nervous?

AVIS

Not a bit. Why should I be nervous?

PHILIP

I'm a little embarrassed. Something embarrassing, somehow, about one's father getting married.

AVIS

I don't think so. (*She sits on couch, picks up magazine and pencil and proceeds to make notes*) Besides, they're not married yet. Maybe Dad's just having her in for inspection.

PHILIP

Is she a *femme fatale,* do you suppose?

AVIS

I wonder. This time Dad seems to have applied the Talley Method with a vengeance. Imagine marrying a patient!

PHILIP

Why? Sensible. If she has nothing more to reveal at least there must be little left to conceal. Shall we show our best side?

AVIS

Didn't know we had one. Let's be natural.

PHILIP

Then she'll never marry Dad.

AVIS

(*Satirically*)

Think we'll be able to adjust ourselves?

PHILIP

If she can, we can. If she can, all I can say is she's highly adjustable.

AVIS

(*Rises*)

How much have you read? (*She goes to telephone.*)

PHILIP

Of our prospective mother's poems? About half.

AVIS

(*She dials a number*)

Well?

PHILIP

Oh, nostalgia in a vacuum. Nicely written. Charming phrasing. What would be called, I believe—sensitive.

AVIS

(*By this time she has her number*)

Hello. . . . Mr. Geist, please, Manfred Geist . . . Miss Talley . . . Avis Talley. . . . Thank you . . . Hello, dear. . . . Look here, Manfred, a rather devastating thing has happened. . . . Dad's bringing a bride home to meet us. . . . Well, a fiancée or intended or whatever you want to call her. . . . It's such a bore because I wanted to get an early start to Washington. . . . Oh, no, I wouldn't think of it. Tonight's the opening session and I wouldn't have you miss it for anything—besides, I'm an officer. You see, darling, the Youth Congress isn't like the Federal Congress—every session is important. . . . Well, come here, will you, and we'll get off as soon as possible. Come right away. . . . Good-bye, darling. (*She hangs up*) He's coming over. We're driving to

Washington. Cy Blodgett's coming with us. We can squeeze you in. Want to come?

PHILIP

No, thanks.

AVIS

Do you like Manfred?

PHILIP

Very much. He's charming—and something very touching about him.

AVIS

Don't pity Manfred. He's been through everything. The rest is velvet. He doesn't know it yet, but I'm going to marry him.

PHILIP

If I didn't pity him before, I do now.

AVIS

No, we'll be wonderful together.

PHILIP

If it isn't too vulgar to inquire, what are you going to marry on?

AVIS

Our youth.

PHILIP

He's twice your age.

AVIS

On our hopes.

PHILIP

A penniless refugee.

AVIS

We've got the future. There'll be a new world.

PHILIP

Undoubtedly. Will it be desirable?

AVIS

I think so.

PHILIP

Don't think Dad will back you in a venture like that!

AVIS

Do you think I'm counting on that? Do you think I'd let *him* support us?

PHILIP

You will if you have to.

AVIS

I'll translate Manfred's books. I'll work. We'll manage. Don't you worry about us!

PHILIP

I'm worried about Manfred. I like him. (*A pause*) One of his books was translated, wasn't it—his prison memoirs? Did anyone buy it?

AVIS

I wish Dad and his bride would hurry up.

PHILIP

Miracle, isn't it? Dad in love! When did he get the time, do you suppose?

AVIS

Between whiffs of anesthetic, while she was on the operating-table, he might have noticed her.

PHILIP

I wonder if he felt he should provide a mother for us? Has that occurred to you?

AVIS

Nonsense. He rushes from duodenum to duodenum. Where would he get the time to think of us? The mystery to me is why, when she got out of the anesthetic, this poetic gal should have consented to marry Dad.

PHILIP

Is that incomprehensible? He's one of the greatest surgeons in America. He's preoccupied, I admit, but he saves people's lives.

AVIS

I wonder. He has a knack of knitting sutures. Very skillful, like tying sailors' knots or fancy embroidering.

PHILIP

You're unfair to Dad.

(CY BLODGETT *comes in, carrying a newspaper which he flourishes portentously. He is about twenty-four. He greets them with an embracing, flamboyant gesture.*)

CY

Well, *mes enfants*. Wonderful news—millennial!

AVIS

Hello, Cy.

PHILIP

How are you, Cy?

CY

It will alter all our lives.

AVIS

For the better?

CY

This makes it possible for you, my dear Avis, to break forever the platinum cord that ties you to your father. For you, my good Philip, to marry your strip-tease artist.

PHILIP

She's not a strip-tease artist. She's a fan dancer.

CY

What's the difference?

AVIS

A fan dancer discards the fan.

CY

You will be able to buy her wondrous fans of Chinese jade. She will be able to discard a fortune in fans. As for me—I shall probably quit Columbia.

AVIS

Come on, Cy—come to the gag.

CY

No gag. For six years I have been killing my leisure with post-graduate work at Columbia. You and Phil have been lured to less innocent diversions. But all that's over. It is finished—we are free!

PHILIP

Are we? I'll bite. How?

CY

Well, if you read this article, cold and statistical, you will find that there is no unemployment in America.

AVIS

Really!

CY

Absolutely. Never has been. There is no unemployment at all. If we are unemployed it is because we are capricious. We're O.K. We're all set. I may even ask for a raise.

PHILIP

You must be getting a good deal now.

CY

Oh, yes. Very decent honorarium, old fellow.

PHILIP

If it isn't too personal, my dear Cy, how much do you get?

CY

(*He drops his voice to a confidential tone*)

Wouldn't want Avis to overhear, old chap; that sort of thing makes Communists . . .

PHILIP

(*Understanding*)

Naturally!

CY

Well, just between you and me—man to man—it runs away up into the zeros.

PHILIP

I'm not surprised. You're worth your weight in zeros.

CY

Thank you, old fellow.

PHILIP

Not at all, old chap. (*They shake hands solemnly.*)

AVIS

Perpetual adolescents!

(*The telephone rings.* CY *picks up book from table and starts to read.* AVIS *starts to answer the phone.*)

PHILIP

(*Jumping up and going to phone*)

That's probably for me. (*Into phone*) Hello . . . Sybil?

I'm sorry, darling . . . I tried to get you before . . . I've got to wait on a bit, but I'll meet you at the Club. Oh, please, Sybil, I couldn't help it, honestly. When I tell you you'll understand. . . .

CY

(*To* AVIS, *as he looks through the book*)

Do you think she'll understand, Avis?

AVIS

If she does, it'll be for the first time.

PHILIP

(*At phone*)

I'll meet you after the supper show and take you to dinner.

CY

What does Sybil wear to go out to dinner in, do you suppose?

AVIS

Oh, she just clicks her costume and sallies forth. (AVIS *makes a gesture of snapping a fan open.*)

PHILIP

(*Still on phone*)

I'll be there right after the supper show. Good-bye, darling. (*He hangs up. He is very angry*) I heard your bright remarks about Sybil . . .

AVIS

All in fun, Philip.

PHILIP

I want to tell you neither of you is in position to patronize Sybil!

CY

Oh, come now, Phil, where's your sense of humor?

AVIS

Don't appeal to the non-existent.

PHILIP

Sybil's supporting herself and three younger sisters. She works like a slave. That's more than any of us do. We're parasites and she's a worker.

CY

I'd do a strip-tease in a minute if anybody'd engage me. I get no offers. (*Puts down poetry book*) What about you, Avis? Let's see. Stand up. Turn around. (AVIS *rises and does a turn*) Take off something. (AVIS *starts to loosen her belt*) Something more strategic. (AVIS *pulls her dress up a little, reaching for her garter.*)

PHILIP

You're too damned bright, both of you. In fact you make me sick! Where the devil is Dad? If he doesn't come in a few minutes I'm leaving anyway—bride or no bride.

CY

Bride? What bride? Whose bride?

AVIS

Dad's.

CY

Really? Congratulations! Who is she?

AVIS

Enid Fuller.

CY

The poet?

AVIS

Yes. Have you read her?

CY

Here and there. Very subtle.

PHILIP

(*He is very morose*)

We're no good—any of us.

CY

Don't be defeatist, Phil.

PHILIP

People like us are in the worst position. If we were downright poor—poverty-stricken—we could go on relief. If we'd learned to use our hands instead of our heads we'd probably be better off. But as it is there's nothing but parasitism—post-graduate courses at Columbia—till our parents die, when we'll probably have to borrow to meet the inheritance tax.

AVIS

All of which is true—but what are you doing about it?

PHILIP

Not deluding myself with the millennium the way you're doing!

AVIS

(*Rises*)

You're a self-indulgent, ineffectual little cry-baby!

CY

(*Rises*)

Avis—moderation!

AVIS

You're sentimental, my dear Philip. Sentimental and inadequate . . .

(ENID FULLER *comes in through archway. She is a very attractive woman of about thirty-five.*)

PHILIP

If you say that again I'll . . .

AVIS

What will you do—strike me?

PHILIP

I'll kill you! I can't bear you, Avis; you bring out the worst in me . . .

(ENID *starts to go.* CY *sees her and tries to stop the fight.*)

AVIS

Well, I don't exactly have to excavate!

PHILIP

One of these days I swear I'll just . . .

(*When* PHILIP *and* AVIS *see* ENID, *they subside quickly.*)

ENID

I'm sorry.

CY

Little family quarrel.

ENID

I'm Enid Fuller. I've been waiting downstairs in the doctor's office—getting courage to come up.

CY

You'll find nothing here but sweetness and light—with a touch of murder. I'm Cy Blodgett.

ENID

(*She shakes hands with him*)

How do you do?

CY

(*Presenting*)

Philip Talley.

PHILIP

Hello.

ENID

Hello, Philip.

PHILIP

(*He has not regained control of himself*)

I'm very angry. I . . .

ENID

Take your time with it!

CY

Avis Talley.

(AVIS *comes to meet her. They shake hands.*)

ENID

Hello, Avis. Your father's told me a great deal about you.

AVIS

How would he know?

(ENID *turns to* CY *for aid.*)

CY

Brother and sister squabble.

PHILIP

She's not my sister.

CY

Now, Phil . . .

AVIS

I was adopted when he was four to be a companion to him!

ENID

Oh?

AVIS

Didn't Father tell you that?

ENID

(*Looking from one to the other*)

I'm sure he's forgotten which one he adopted.

CY

That's very graceful.

AVIS

Where is the bridegroom—may I ask?

ENID

(*Amused*)

You mean your father? The bridegroom was called on a case at the last minute . . .

AVIS

Already?

ENID

He wanted to call you to make another arrangement but I wouldn't let him. I thought I'd take the plunge by myself.

AVIS

That gives you a rough idea of what you'll be in for.

ENID

I've discounted that.

AVIS

We never see Father. He breakfasts too early and dines too late.

ENID

I'll try to arrange for you to meet him.

AVIS

I think the conversation would lag.

ENID

(*With a rather desperate, at once hopeful and helpless look at* CY)

Perhaps Mr. Blodgett would come and fill in the gaps!

CY

(*Gone for her*)

Mrs. Fuller . . .

ENID

Miss Fuller.

CY

Oh, I'm sorry. Miss Fuller . . .

ENID

Yes, Mr. Blodgett . . .

CY

If your commitment to Dr. Talley is not irrevocable . . .

ENID

(*Taking courage, plays along on nerve*)

Very few things in life are irrevocable, Mr. Blodgett.

CY

Will you consider me?

ENID

I'm doing it. I'm doing it now.

CY

I have an A.B. and an M.A. and in a year I'll be a Ph.D. You can't tell what I'll have when I'm fifty. Will you share them with me?

ENID

Am I worthy?

CY

I feel in you, Mrs. Fuller . . .

ENID

Miss Fuller.

CY

Why do I keep calling you Mrs. Fuller?

ENID

I wonder.

CY

I'll look that up tomorrow, Miss Fuller!

ENID

In what?

CY

Where were we?

ENID

You were sharing your degrees with me. If I were predatory I might take advantage of you.

CY

My impulse with you is to throw discretion to the winds. Avis, I am free of you at last! (*Turns to* ENID) Up to now I have been in love with Avis. (*Again to* AVIS) I realize now I haven't been too happy with you, Avis. Too much ideology, too little sex. (*To* ENID) Thank you, Miss Fuller. Thank you very much.

ENID

You should have told me *you* were committed. I'm sorry, Avis. May I call you Avis?

AVIS

Certainly.

ENID

I didn't know about you and Cy.

AVIS

It's all right with me.

ENID

I'm sure it isn't. It couldn't be. Cy is too sympathetic altogether for you to feel that way. Wait. Be patient. He will return to you.

CY

(*To* AVIS)

Never!

ENID

Oh, dear Cy. I feel you cooling off already. I can feel it. I could sense it by the intensity with which you just said "Never." But it's been charming! I've heard of love at first sight. I've even written of it but I've never experienced it. Thank you, Cy!

AVIS

What about Dad? Wasn't that first sight?

ENID

No, I don't think so. Have any of you ever been his patient?

CY

We can't afford him, Miss Fuller.

ENID

I'll be glad to stake you—it's a wonderful experience.

AVIS

How is he when you're not his patient?

PHILIP

Don't listen to her, Miss Fuller . . .

ENID

Call me Enid. Please do.

PHILIP

(*Awkwardly*)

Thanks!

ENID

What were you saying, Philip?

PHILIP

(*Points to* AVIS)

Don't listen to her—to what she says—she'd try to break you up. She hates Father.

ENID

Now, Avis, that can't be true.

AVIS

I think if I knew him I wouldn't like him!

ENID

Why?

AVIS

Why?

ENID

Tell me why.

AVIS

(*Marshaling her thoughts exactly*)

For one thing, he doesn't know and doesn't care not only about what goes on in this house but in the world at large. His outlook is limited to his specialty. He can't see beyond the end of his duodenum.

ENID

If yours were annoying you—as mine did recently—you might be grateful for that concentration.

PHILIP

Avis is a violent Red, though, like most Reds, she won't admit it. Any other shade bores her.

AVIS

(*She jumps up, speaks passionately*)

That's right. That's easy. Red. Smear the epithet and finish me. That's all you have to do. Settles every argument.

CY

Tell me, Miss Fuller, what do you think of the Government's policy of buying Mexican silver?

AVIS

Make fun of me, Cy. That won't alter me and it won't alter the facts.

PHILIP

Wouldn't you like some tea, Miss Fuller?

ENID

I'd love some.

PHILIP

I'll see if I can jog up Mary. She's willing but absent-minded.

ENID

Thank you.

(PHILIP *goes out. A moment's pause.*)

CY

(*Trying to ease the silence*)

How does it feel, Miss Fuller, to become a mother overnight, as it were?

ENID

Very exciting.

CY

Ever happen to you before?

ENID

No—it's the first time. (*She rises, looks at* AVIS *and smiles, hoping to make friends*) Tell me, Avis—what does Philip do exactly?

CY

He's in love. He's in love with a strip-tease artist at a night club in the Village. Only he doesn't like her called that. He prefers her to be called a fan dancer. We all have our odd little vanities.

ENID

(*To* AVIS)

Do you know her?

CY

None of us has met her. He holds her close. What do you suppose they talk about when they're alone, Avis?

AVIS

I haven't the faintest idea.

CY

He must get a great kick out of seeing her dressed! He's about the only one in town.

(PHILIP *comes back.*)

PHILIP

(*To* ENID)

In just a minute.

ENID

Thank you very much. Come—sit by me, Philip.

PHILIP

Thank you. I've got to be leaving in a minute—Dad or no Dad.

CY

We've been telling her about your romance, Phil.

PHILIP

(*His back up*)

Oh!

ENID

What's her name, Phil?

PHILIP

Sybil.

ENID

Sybil! What a lovely name. And for a dancer—curiously right! Won't you let me meet her, Philip?

PHILIP

(*Responding*)

Yes, *you* can meet her.

ENID

Thank you. We'll arrange it. Will you bring her to my apartment?

PHILIP

(*Almost defiantly, to show the others*)

Yes. I will.

CY

(*To* ENID)

Now Avis's love-life is something else again.

(AVIS *takes a step toward* CY, *threateningly.*)

ENID

Really?

CY

Manfred Geist.

ENID

(*Quite surprised*)

Really?

CY

You've heard of him?

ENID

The author of *My Prison Year*?

AVIS

(*Blushing with pleasure*)

Yes. You know him then?

ENID

Well, I haven't met him. But I've read his book.

CY

So you were the one!

AVIS

(*Speaks eagerly*)

Did you like it?

ENID

It's a wonderful book.

AVIS

He's a wonderful person.

CY

He's nearly fifty.

AVIS

(*Hotly*)

What's that got to do with it?

CY

That tells her how old he is.

(MARY *enters carrying tea tray.*)

MARY

I believe Mr. Geist just came in, Miss Avis.

AVIS

Oh, thank you, Mary! (*She runs out.*)

(PHILIP *picks up tea table, puts it in front of* ENID.)

CY

You see the way things are, Miss Fuller. Before this poetic refugee came on the scene, I was making a good, slow progress. But since he's appeared, Avis won't even stop long enough to say "No" to me. I wish this damned war would end so that Manfred could go back to Europe.

MARY

I'm so glad about you, Miss Fuller.

ENID

Thank you, Mary.

MARY

It will be nice to have a woman in the house. (*A moment*) Everything all right?

ENID

(*Smiling at her*)

Couldn't be better!

MARY

Good!

ENID

(*As she picks up tea pot*)

I'll pour. May I?

PHILIP

Of course.

(AVIS *comes in followed by* MANFRED GEIST.)

Hello, Manfred.

CY

Hello, Manfred. (*He rises and shakes hands with* MANFRED. ENID *rises.*)

MANFRED

(*As he shakes hand*)

Hello, Cy.

AVIS

This is Miss Fuller—my step-mother-to-be. Mr. Manfred Geist.

(*They shake hands.*)

ENID

I am very glad to meet you, Mr. Geist.

MANFRED

Thank you. I am proud.

AVIS

Manfred has heard of you!

MANFRED

I have done more than that. I have read you.

ENID

Really?

MANFRED

With admiration. With envy.

ENID

(*Pleased and embarrassed*)

Thank you.

AVIS

That's a tribute—from a great poet like Manfred.

ENID

It is indeed. Some tea?

MANFRED

Thank you.

PHILIP

(*Rising*)

Well, I'm afraid I've got to go! Tell Dad I'm sorry, will you please, but I really couldn't wait. Anyway, I've met you, haven't I, and that's the main point.

ENID

Yes.

PHILIP

(*Shyly*)

Well—good-bye.

ENID

(*Offering him her hand*)

Good-bye, Philip.

(ENID *and* PHILIP *shake hands.*)

PHILIP

When are you coming here to live?

ENID

Well, as soon as I can.

PHILIP

Oh, come before that.

ENID

Thank you very much, Philip. I hope I shall see you soon again and that I shall meet Sybil.

PHILIP

I'd love to bring her—when nobody else is home but you. Good-bye, Manfred.

MANFRED

Good-bye, Philip.

CY

So long, Phil.

PHILIP

So long.

CY

Catch a garment on the wing and bring it to me for a scarf. Will you, Philip? I like vermilion.

(*With a bitter look at him,* PHIL *goes out.*)

AVIS

I'm afraid we've got to be going too, Manfred. (*She takes* MANFRED'S *cup*) It's a seven-hour drive to Washington.

CY

Why don't we take the train? With the three of us your

Ford'll be none too comfortable. Have you ridden it, Manfred?

MANFRED

I have!

AVIS

If we don't mind, you shouldn't. What've you got to do?

CY

Just run home for my white tie.

AVIS

Well, run. We'll pick you up in half an hour. I'll ring your door-bell twice. If you're not there, we'll go without you.

CY

You see me, Miss Fuller, dominated, badgered.

ENID

Perhaps discipline is what you need, Mr. Blodgett.

CY

No, Miss Fuller, I need sympathy, indulgence, appreciation. (*Moves closer to* ENID) May I come to you one day and give you the data to help you to understand me!

ENID

I'd be delighted.

CY

Thank you. Gosh, it's wonderful to have an alternative!

(*During the following conversation* MANFRED *listens, amused.*)

ENID

What an odd boy! Really an original.

AVIS

He clowns, but he's got a good brain if he'd only use it.

ENID

On what?

AVIS

On something constructive instead of collecting useless degrees at Columbia. You see, Miss Fuller . . .

ENID

Call me Enid. Please do. . . .

AVIS

I'd love to. You see, Enid . . .

ENID

Yes.

AVIS

Oh, how can I talk to you?

ENID

Well, you might try . . .

AVIS

You're very nice. One can see that only . . . (AVIS *stops awkwardly.*)

ENID

What?

AVIS

I mean how can I talk to you when I don't know what your prejudices are? Where you interests lie. What your background is.

ENID

Why can't you assume that I'm a human being? That is to say that I am selfish and egotistical, as it is very difficult not to be but that I am aware of it, that at my best I want to understand people and not hurt them, even help them, that if I had my way we should communicate everywhere affectionately—and even where possible, lovingly.

AVIS

I am sure you are well-meaning. I am sure you are benevolent. But you see—benevolence isn't enough.

ENID

(*Humorously*)

It seems not to be.

AVIS

People in your generation had a chance. We haven't. In one way or another we're on the dole—all of us. Is that to be our future? There are millions of young people like me in this country who want their rights—not a dole. People pretend we're fanatics and cranks. They won't face what we're about. We're misrepresented. In novels and plays the charm is always reserved for the aging reactionaries. We're supposed to be ungracious and horrid . . . And why? Because we want to live. We want to live on our own. We don't want to be killed in wars for objectives that aren't our objectives. We want decency and truth. (*She stops. There is a silence*) I'm sorry.

ENID

Why?

AVIS

One shouldn't express oneself.

ENID

Why not?

AVIS

Manfred says I— Are you angry with me, Manfred?

MANFRED

Of course not.

AVIS

Are you ready to go?

MANFRED

Oh, yes. (*He rises. To* ENID) I'm looking forward to this trip to Washington. I've never been there.

ENID

It's a lovely city. You'll like it, I think.

AVIS

I'll be ready in a minute. Excuse me?

ENID

Certainly.

AVIS

Will you wait?

ENID

I will indeed.

AVIS

Thank you.

MANFRED

Don't forget the book you told me about.

AVIS

I won't. (*She goes out and upstairs.*)

MANFRED

I'm not, you know.

ENID

I beg your pardon?

MANFRED

I'm not the great poet Avis thinks me. I have written poetry and I have published poetry. But I am not a poet.

ENID

You are modest.

MANFRED

It is not modesty. It is criticism. As a matter of fact, you are an authentic poet—I am not.

ENID

You've really read my verses?

MANFRED

I know some of them by heart.

ENID

Really!

MANFRED

Shall I recite one?

ENID

Please not.

MANFRED

You said just now that each of us is vain and egotistical. How true! My vanity is to let Avis believe that I am a great man. Like most people reading a foreign language she is less critical than she would be in her own.

ENID

I cannot quite believe that a reputation which crosses the Atlantic has no authenticity.

MANFRED

It is an adventitious reputation!

ENID

After all, I've read your book. I was fascinated. You headed a putsch in Bavaria against the first Nazis, didn't you?

MANFRED

Yes.

ENID

And the poems you wrote in prison—I read them in translation—I was very moved by them.

MANFRED

The poems had anguish and they had sincerity but these are not enough. They became famous not because they were remarkable but because I was young and they were written in prison. All these years I have had to sustain a reputation for greatness when I have only that most frequent of commodities—talent.

ENID

Courage is a kind of poetry. A high kind. A flouting of the Fates.

MANFRED

It's extraordinary, really . . . It's extraordinary . . .

ENID

What?

MANFRED

It's astonishing how under the shadow of the great tragedy that hovers over the world, one's personal tragedy can still make itself felt—insistent—insistent as a toothache.

ENID

Perhaps that's lucky. That indicates we haven't given up. That indicates we are alive. That defies regimentation.

MANFRED

You make me feel better. Thank you. Thank you very much.

ENID

For what?

MANFRED

You have given me some sort of excuse, some sort of justification. You ease my conscience.

ENID

Is it stained with guilt?

MANFRED

In a way . . .

ENID

As which of us isn't!

MANFRED

You know I am happy about you—that you are entering this family.

ENID

Thank you.

MANFRED

You'll be good for Avis. She needs a woman like you near her.

ENID

I like her very much.

MANFRED

I feel very concerned about her. She may seem to you difficult but, believe me, she is honest—she is wonderful.

ENID

I can see that.

MANFRED

For some obscure reason Avis is in love with me. Perhaps it is because I am a victim of the force she detests. It is her gesture of defiance. I am going with her to this meeting. I'm eager to hear her speak, to see her on the platform before these thousands of people . . .

ENID

A Jeanne d'Arc without armor . . .

MANFRED

Yes—I know I should stop her from loving me. I should disappear. And yet I am pleased. I am singularly pleased. The grinning little ego whispers: You are a penniless exile. You are no longer young—and yet an exquisite young girl is in love with you. It must be that you are not dead yet! (ENID *rises and goes to table for cigarette box*) I find it extraordinarily easy to talk to you. To be frank with you. Perhaps it is because I know your verses. By knowing your verses I know you.

ENID

(*Offers him a cigarette*)

Do you write still?

MANFRED

Oh, yes—one writes . . .

ENID

In English or in German?

MANFRED

(*Takes cigarette*)

Naturally—in German.

ENID

You speak so well—you might easily, I should think . . .

MANFRED

When I get a pen into my hand, I find it is German that I write. Avis is my translator. It is part of her crusade.

ENID

I am sure Avis will do it well. I have confidence in Avis.

MANFRED

And if she does, what then? Who wants to read a minor German writer? Surely the world is too busy for that.

ENID

The minor writers are often the most endearing—or so I often console myself. Sometimes—in fact very often—in fact nearly all the time—one may prefer Herrick to Milton.

MANFRED

Or Heine or Goethe.

ENID

Decidedly.

MANFRED

Now all one has to do is to be Heine.

ENID

For a writer to be bereft of his speech is a hard fate! To have mastered the intimacies of a language; to have achieved the signature of personality—and then not to be able to use it—that must be the greatest frustration of all.

MANFRED

Oh, there are a few giants and they tower above the divisions of language. They are international although they too have lost their natural audience in their own tongue.

ENID

I have thought of this—will you believe me when I tell you that I have thought often of this?

MANFRED

You are a poet and therefore no pain is foreign to you. Your imagination spares you nothing!

ENID

We live in a time when the truest voices are struck dumb by the loudest!

MANFRED

Avis thinks Communism will cure everything. I wonder. How shrewd our Leader is! There is something devastating in his propaganda that has appealed to the Fifth Column that lurks in every soul.

ENID

That I deny. That I repudiate.

MANFRED

I was cynical—till now. I believed that—till now!

(AVIS *comes in with an overnight bag.*)

AVIS

Oh! I'm sorry! I seem to have broken into a mood.

ENID

I am grateful to you already, Avis—for letting me know Mr. Geist. Please let me meet more of your friends.

AVIS

Well—shall we go?

MANFRED

I am ready. You are leaving Miss Fuller alone?

AVIS

If she marries Father, she'll have to get used to that.

ENID

I am used to it already. I've been used to it for years.

MANFRED

Miss Fuller . . .

ENID

Yes?

MANFRED

I should like you to meet my daughter Ingrid.

ENID

I'd love to.

MANFRED

Thank you.

ENID

What shall I tell your father, Avis?

AVIS

He won't ask, but if he does, tell him I've gone to Washington.

ENID

When will you be back?

AVIS

In a few days.

ENID

You must promise to tell me all about it.

AVIS

(*Turns to* ENID)

If you're interested, I'll be glad to tell you.

MANFRED

If Avis is too busy, I'll be glad to report it to you. I specialize in Youth Movements. I was nearly killed in one.

ENID

Let us hope you find this one more merciful. Good-bye, Mr. Geist. Pleasant journey.

MANFRED

Thank you.

AVIS

Enid, when you do marry Father I wish you'd get him to replace some of this furniture. Some of it comes from Dad's old waiting room. We call it the Manic Depressive style. On that sofa have sat all the patients Father killed before he hit on the Talley Method. Father can't bear to throw anything away—not only an old idea but even an old sofa. It would break his heart.

(MANFRED *manages to exchange a quizzical look with* ENID *and to get one word in before* AVIS *marches him out.*)

MANFRED

Oh, come now, Avis, you will admit that at least Miss Fuller is an innovation!

AVIS

(*With a quick look at* ENID)

Come on, Manfred! (*She goes out.*)

MANFRED

(*Smiling*)

Courage! (*He follows* AVIS *out.*)

(*Left alone,* ENID *has a reaction. She hasn't realized how much of an ordeal it was for her to face those children. She sinks down in the center chair, her arms falling limp beside her, as if she had been through vio-*

lent exercise. Then she pulls herself together a little and looks around the room. She feels a certain unreality. She rises, looks at the Manic Depressive sofa, then turns and walks around looking at everything curiously. She takes off her hat, moves down to fireplace and spies a bit of marble bric-a-brac that makes her shudder. She turns, puts her hat on the desk. The office door opens and AXTON *rushes in.* ENID *is overjoyed. She rushes to him. They embrace warmly.)*

ENID

Darling . . .

AXTON

Terribly sorry . . .

ENID

I'm so glad to see you!

AXTON

It couldn't be helped.

ENID

Thank God, you've come at last!

AXTON

Forty minutes late.

ENID

Those forty minutes!

AXTON

Did you meet them?

ENID

(*They let each other go*)

I did indeed.

AXTON

Was it an ordeal for you?

ENID

I didn't realize how much—till it was over.

AXTON

Sorry it had to happen this way.

ENID

I'm glad it did. I broke the ice. It's all right now, but I'd built up in my own mind such a hazard over meeting your children. Well, I jumped it. I did it on nerve, but I jumped it. Whew, Axton! You gave me no idea—they're so bright—they're so keen—took all I had to keep up with them. Think I did it, Axton. They'll never know what it cost me. But I kept up with 'em! (*A moment*) I hope!

AXTON

Good.

ENID

(*She looks at him with great concern*)

What is it, darling?

AXTON

Bit tired.

ENID

You look worn out.

AXTON

Am rather. Lost a patient. Seldom happens to me.

ENID

Something go wrong?

AXTON

No. Everything was right. Worked perfectly. But we miscalculated the patient's resistance. Died under the anesthetic. Some weakness somewhere. We didn't detect it. The postmortem will show it.

ENID

Who was he—your patient?

AXTON

It was a woman.

ENID

What was her name?

AXTON

Robinson, I think. Mrs. Robinson.

ENID

With you Death is anonymous, isn't it? Like war.

AXTON

You know, Enid . . .

ENID

Yes, dear?

AXTON

I worked as well as I ever did—really as quickly and

surely as I ever did in my life. Everything was right and yet she died. It seldom happens to me. Some weakness somewhere.

ENID

As you made no slip—you can't blame yourself, can you?

AXTON

Shouldn't have operated.

ENID

If you hadn't—would she have lived?

AXTON

Not long. But it's her dying on the table I don't like.

ENID

(*Delicately*)

You wish she had done it—independently?

AXTON

Some weakness—somewhere. . . .

(ENID *puts her hands on his shoulders.*)

ENID

Well, darling, people do have weaknesses and often these weaknesses kill them. You can't remedy that.

AXTON

(*Shaking his head gloomily*)

She had no stamina.

ENID

You must forgive her, darling. She probably meant well.

AXTON

(*Has scarcely heard her*)

Poor diagnosis! Well . . . ! (*He shakes it off finally, looks at her, smiles at her. She smiles back at him. They rest momentarily on a little plateau of sympathetic understanding. She sits on arm of chair and puts her arm around him*) Nice to have you here, Enid.

ENID

Is it? Is it really?

AXTON

Nice to come home and find you.

ENID

(*Tenderly, murmurs*)

Axton . . .

AXTON

You'll be happy, I think.

ENID

I'm sure.

AXTON

How did you get on actually—with the kids? Did you mind them?

ENID

On the contrary. I like them very much. Although . . .

AXTON

What?

ENID

One thing about them I couldn't quite understand.

AXTON

(*Dryly*)

There are many things about them *I* can't understand.

ENID

Their attitude about you—they don't seem to realize how wonderful you are.

AXTON

If they thought I was wonderful, it would worry me quite a lot!

ENID

As a matter of fact, I felt rather sorry for them.

AXTON

Why?

ENID

They feel betrayed. They're cynical. They're disillusioned.

AXTON

They're weak.

ENID

I didn't feel that. I felt potential strength.

AXTON

Look at Philip!

ENID

I liked him so much. He's charming!

AXTON

These days, I'm afraid, charm isn't enough.

ENID

What about Philip?

AXTON

Funked medical school.

ENID

Didn't he work hard enough?

AXTON

I didn't say he flunked. He *funked*.

ENID

How do you mean?

AXTON

Couldn't stand the dissecting-room. Walked out. Quit!

ENID

Doesn't it indicate, perhaps, that he's not suited to medicine as a career?

AXTON

Not at all. Most students get a bit nauseated in the dissecting-room. They stick it out, that's all.

ENID

It's a bitter disappointment to you, isn't it?

AXTON

(*Shortly. He sits forward in his chair*)

Yes. It is.

ENID

What have you done about it?

AXTON

What is there to do? I've talked to the boy. I've argued with him. He won't go back. He won't accept what I can offer him. Where there's no character, Enid, you can't supply it.

ENID

Supposing he went back; supposing he stuck it out and were mediocre, how would you feel about that?

AXTON

The Talleys are not mediocre! My father, I think I've told you, was a distinguished Roentgenologist. His father was a country doctor in Wyoming. Philip would have been the fourth in an unbroken line. He's broken it. Here's a boy with a useful career set for him. A tradition set for him. He'd have inherited my practice. Didn't want it. When I'm dead there'll be no Dr. Talley. It'll be the first time since 1797. We reach back to the eighteenth century.

ENID

There'll be the Talley Method.

AXTON

Yes. Till it's superseded.

ENID

(*Lightly*)

What a passion for survival!

AXTON

That's instinctive, don't you think? Why do you write poetry?

ENID

Because I can't help it!

AXTON

Maybe if the impulse were analyzed, that is what it would be found to be.

ENID

I wonder. Am I so vain? To make yourself legible to your contemporaries is difficult enough—to chat with the future positively foolhardy!

(*A moment's pause.*)

AXTON

How'd you get on with Avis?

ENID

I liked her especially.

AXTON

Did you?

(*A moment's pause.*)

ENID

Axton . . .

AXTON

Yes?

ENID

You don't see much of your children, do you?

AXTON

Well, you know how it is, Enid. I have a large practice. It keeps me going.

ENID

I think they feel it.

AXTON

Do they? Do they really?

ENID

They feel you're remote from them. I can see that.

AXTON

As a matter of fact, Enid, you needn't worry about the children—not to excess. They won't be with us long.

ENID

Really! They seem so well!

AXTON

(*Literally*)

I don't mean physically. They're in excellent condition physically.

ENID

That's good!

AXTON

What I mean is that I have every expectation that they'll soon get married.

ENID

Oh?

AXTON

There's some foolish young fellow sparking around Avis now . . .

ENID

Cy?

AXTON

His name is Blodgett, I believe.

ENID

That's Cy. And sparking is mild.

AXTON

They'll probably get married. . . .

ENID

(*Innocently*)

You think so?

AXTON

(*Grimly*)

I'll probably have to support them, but it'll be worth it.

ENID

(*Unable to quench her delight in her superior knowledge*)

Oh, my darling, wonderful Axton!

AXTON

(*Surprised*)

What's the matter now?

ENID

This brings you all the closer to me.

AXTON

What does?

ENID

Never mind.

AXTON

(*A bit suspicious*)

These freshets of endearment are so—so unpredictable!

ENID

You'll be perpetually inundated—make up your mind to that. But now tell me about Philip. Is he going to get married too?

AXTON

I'm hoping so. He's interested in somebody. I've given him several strong hints. I know she's interested in him!

ENID

Sybil?

AXTON

Sybil? Who is Sybil?

ENID

Who's yours?

AXTON

Pat Ackerman, Rodney Ackerman's daughter. He's a patient of mine, very rich. As Phil hasn't either a job or a career, he might as well marry money. In any case you may have a reasonable expectancy that you won't be bothered with either of the children very long. After they've both gone, we can have this house to ourselves.

ENID

(*She puts her arms around him*)

Oh, my poor darling!

AXTON

What is it now?

ENID

Nothing.

AXTON

Well, when you say "my poor darling" in that tone, I naturally conclude it *is* something.

ENID

It's just that I'm bewildered.

AXTON

About what?

ENID

About your relations with your children. You seem to know so little about each other.

AXTON

It isn't my fault.

ENID

(*Frankly*)

It must be, Axton—at least partly.

AXTON

I've tried, God knows.

ENID

Try again.

AXTON

Do you think so?

ENID

I would, dear, really. I'd make an effort. Do it for me, will you, darling?

AXTON

Well, perhaps I will.

ENID

(*Chiding him affectionately*)

Come now, I see you filing it away in your mind. You won't do it.

AXTON

I will, I promise.

ENID

(*She puts her arm through his*)

Darling. You are a darling. I'm so proud of you, Axton— You know what I love?— To take you out to dinner, to show you off to my friends, to see you sitting there, silent and unapproachable in the welter of magnified small-talk, a Sphinx among the innuendoes . . .

AXTON

Didn't care much for the literati you introduced me to. Those few dinners you took me to—I was bored.

ENID

You made that evident!

AXTON

Lot of chatter. Your friends may be clever and all that. They may write well and all that, but they don't really know anything. Lot of chatter. I never know what they're talking about and I don't care.

ENID

Darling! Never, never did I love you so much as that night at the dinner-party at Waddington's!

AXTON

Waddington! What's he so famous for? He struck me as trivial.

ENID

(*Slyly*)

He made a *mot* about you.

AXTON

(*Not interested*)

Did he?

ENID

Prompted by your unbroken silence at his dinner.

AXTON

(*Still not interested*)

Really?

ENID

Is the Talley Method, he wanted to know, for lip-reading?

AXTON

Is that funny?

ENID

Not very.

AXTON

Too much talk everywhere.

ENID

I agree.

AXTON

Cant. Everywhere. Speeches. Phrases. Imprecise. Untested generalizations!

ENID

Well, my little circle of sophisticated pals is inclined to cruelty a bit. You're so *kind,* Axton. (*She looks at him*) I could cry when I think how kind you've been to me.

AXTON

Oh, nonsense!

ENID

One has to have been your patient to know how wonderful you are really.

AXTON

Don't be deceived by my professional manner!

ENID

Your infinite care, your solicitude, your *patience*. How wonderfully kind you were! How strong and kind.

AXTON

My job!

ENID

Yes. Your job. How superbly you did it. How the nurses adored you. Just today, Axton . . .

AXTON

What happened today?

ENID

Well, I'd just rung the door-bell on the way up to meet your children. I got stage fright about it suddenly. I thought: "Oh, my dear, what will I say to them? Supposing they hate me." To pull myself together I walked into your waiting-room to sit down for a bit . . .

AXTON

Well?

ENID

There was an old woman sitting there. She was waiting for instructions from your nurse. We got to talking. We got to talking about you.

AXTON

(*Simply*)

Hope she didn't give me away!

ENID

She blessed you, Axton. (AXTON *makes a deprecatory sound*) She told me how you saved her husband's life—a motorman on the Third Avenue El.

AXTON

Oh, Mrs. Pink!

ENID

Yes. Odd name for her. She blessed you. You'd never taken a penny from her, she said—you kept coming to her tenement, countless visits, treating her husband as if he were a millionaire. She said you couldn't possibly have taken more pains—"Not," said Mrs. Pink, "if my husband was Mr. Rockeyfelley."

AXTON

I soak people like you in order to treat for nothing people like the Pinks!

ENID

Which reminds me—I've never had a bill from you.

AXTON

(*Dryly*)

I don't want to add to my liabilities.

ENID

Darling!

AXTON

You keep talking about what I did for you. What about what you've done for me?

ENID

(*Tremulous*)

Have I, Axton?

AXTON

I was lonely, Enid. I didn't know it. It's difficult for me to say these things. . . .

ENID

Try! You've never told me, as a matter of fact. . . .

AXTON

Haven't I? I thought I had.

ENID

Darling!

AXTON

My life is quite a grind. I work till I'm exhausted. Then I take a holiday. But holidays make me vaguely unhappy. They rest me but they upset me. I know now why. I become conscious then that I'm alone. My next will be with you. That's wonderful.

ENID

(*She puts her arms around him*)

You need never be lonely again, darling. Never again.

AXTON

Have I told you now?

ENID

You've conveyed it!

AXTON

I love you, Enid. Yes. It's true.

(*A silence. They look at each other.*)

ENID

It's a miracle. After all my wanderings—emotionally, I mean—to have found you. It's a miracle. Do you know, Axton . . .

AXTON

What?

ENID

There's something I haven't told you.

AXTON

What?

ENID

That before I met you, before I came under your care—I had reached such a state of mind that I wanted to die.

AXTON

(*Surprised*)

Really, why?

ENID

I had a kind of—sickness of life.

AXTON

(*Flatly*)

Physical.

ENID

(*She turns to him*)

Unfortunately, no. Spiritual.

AXTON

Well, the fact is you did emerge. And you seemed to like it.

ENID

That was you. You gave me a reason for living—a new lease on life. I've got to tell you, Axton. You've got to know—what a fragile creature I really am!

AXTON

(*Indulgently*)

Well, then—tell me!

ENID

When I went into the hospital—I had reached the end of my rope.

AXTON

You see you were mistaken.

ENID

I had been hovering on the brink of psychoanalysis, but I couldn't quite take the plunge. I was inhibited somehow about embarking on an endless career of audible introspection.

AXTON

Quite right!

ENID

Nevertheless, I saw no way out. I was sick of myself and of life. . . .

AXTON

Was it that nephew of yours that was killed in the plane?

ENID

It was beyond even that, deeper even than that. How sick I was of the endlessly swinging arcs of my own imaginations! Robert's death, it is true, became a symbol to me of what the machines were doing to young life everywhere. What were my little subtleties, the thin line of communication I was trying to establish? What if I did establish it? The people I try to reach are of the same mind as I am. Could I ever affect the others? Probably not. The same kind of people talk to each other—and what are we in this world of screaming death and swooping machines? (*She puts her hand in his*) You see I *am* weak, darling. When I was told I had this illness, I was glad. I prayed it would do for me what I lacked the initiative to do for myself.

AXTON

(*He pats her hand*)

You're too introspective.

ENID

Occupational disease!

AXTON

What's accomplished by that sort of mooning about?

ENID

Behind it, I'm afraid, there was something personal, intensely personal.

AXTON

Oh?

ENID

Behind most abstract griefs, there is a core of personal unhappiness. I've made several bad choices, Axton—in love.

AXTON

(*Brusquely*)

Don't want to hear about 'em. Stick to the present, which is myself.

ENID

I will, Axton. I promise you that. (*A moment*) You know,

darling, lying there in the hospital, convalescing, waiting for your step in the corridor—I composed a poem to you!

AXTON

Oh, did you? You never let me see it.

ENID

I never wrote it down. I composed it in my head. I think I could write it from memory. I believe it's the loveliest poem I never wrote.

AXTON

What was it about?

ENID

Your encompassing skill, the swift virtuosity of your healing skill. I thought: While you despair, he saves. The areas sick and lost he reclaims. I thought: Here is a way of life, free and constructive and clearly good. Do many of your patients fall in love with you, Axton?

AXTON

They do while they're weak. . . .

ENID

(*With a quick smile at him*)

My weakness persists—rather, it's supplanted by your strength. Please kiss me. (*He kisses her. They embrace warmly*) You know, darling, it seems to me now that always before—when I thought I had found love . . .

AXTON

I thought we weren't going to talk about that!

ENID

No, but this is what I want to tell you: It seems to me now that there was always a premonition of doubt. This is the first time—this is the first time, darling, that I feel secure—this is the first time I feel completely—at home. I'm home.

AXTON

Yes, of course. You are home.

ENID

It's what we all want deep down, isn't it, Axton?

AXTON

I suppose so.

ENID

At this moment particularly, when we're all on the verge of an abyss, it's such a blessing—to know: This at least is mine, this I can count on, this will not fail me.

(AXTON *kisses her. While he is thus engaged,* MARY *comes in through the archway. Embarrassed at having intruded on this tender scene, she knocks on the archway.* AXTON *turns quickly, a bit embarrassed.*)

AXTON

Come in. Come in, Mary.

MARY

Dinner is served, Doctor.

AXTON

All right, Mary. We'll be right down. This is Miss Fuller. (*He turns and sees* ENID *is still kneeling. His embarrassment returns.*)

ENID

Mary and I have met.

MARY

Indeed we have!

AXTON

Where's Philip?

MARY

He's dining out.

AXTON

Where's Avis?

MARY

Miss Avis has gone to Washington.

AXTON

What's she doing in Washington?

MARY

It's a big meeting!

AXTON

(*To* ENID)

More palaver! (*To* MARY *again*) We shall want a cocktail, Mary.

MARY

Yes. Edward made your favorite—a dikkeree. (MARY *goes out.*)

ENID

(*Going to* AXTON *and taking his hands gaily*)

Dikkeree. She pronounces it like a nursery rhyme. Dikkeree-dikkeree-dock . . . Oh, darling, I feel very gay suddenly. Don't you? I have great reserves of gaiety—you release them.

AXTON

You mustn't overdo!

ENID

You give me confidence, and you can't really be gay without confidence. I'm terrifically up and down, Axton. You're not, are you? How can I keep on an even keel, darling? Will you help me to do that? Will you be my compass?

AXTON

(*Patiently*)

A compass does not keep you at an even keel!

ENID

What does?

AXTON

The nautical engineers have developed—stabilizing instruments.

ENID

What are they called?

AXTON

Gyroscopes.

ENID

Will you be my gyroscope? Doesn't seem right, somehow. No, I'd rather have you for my compass. Accurate or not, you're going to be my compass. Come on, darling. Let's get to those dikkerees. I feel like getting a bit tight, don't you? (*She takes his arm and starts walking out with him.*)

AXTON

(*Affectionately and yet with a touch of professional severity*)

Cocktails are not particularly good for you.

ENID

(*As they go out*)

Oh, now, darling. Why should I be prudent when I'm marrying the Talley Method?

Curtain

ACT TWO

ACT TWO

The same as Act One. A few days later. Afternoon.

AXTON *comes in. He looks around the room; he has an almost guilty feeling at being home at this hour of the day. He rings the bell for* MARY *twice. His eye catches the* New Masses *on the telephone table. He picks it up, looks at it and into it and throws it down violently.* MARY *comes in. She can't believe her eyes.*

MARY

Doctor . . .

AXTON

Hello, Mary.

MARY

Are you ill?

AXTON

Why should I be ill?

MARY

Home at this time of day! What's wrong, Doctor?

AXTON

Nothing's wrong, Mary. Nothing at all. Had a little break between appointments. Thought I'd come home, that's all. What's wrong with that?

MARY

(*Wondering*)

First break you've had in twenty years. Well, well!

AXTON

(*Self-consciously*)

Children home?

MARY

I don't know. I think Mr. Phil's home.

AXTON

Where is he?

MARY

In his room I think.

AXTON

Ask him if he can come down to see me, will you, Mary?

MARY

Has he done something wrong, Doctor?

AXTON

No, he hasn't. What makes you ask an idiotic question like that?

MARY

(*Worried*)

Go easy on him, Doctor.

AXTON

For God's sake, Mary, go and get him down here, will you?

MARY

Phil means well. That boy's got a sweet nature. He's my pet.

AXTON

That does not ingratiate him to me! Go up and get him.

MARY

He was his mother's pet, too.

AXTON

Mary! (*She turns and goes out.* AXTON'S *mission of good will has not had a happy start. He has to fight to regain control of himself.* MARY'S *surprise at seeing him at this untoward hour has dramatized for him rather the justice of* ENID'S *charge that he has neglected his home and his children. But he masters his irritation. His eye catches the* New Masses *on the floor. As a symbol of his contrition, he picks it up, smoothes it out and lays it gently on the desk. But as he does so, something else strikes his eye—some violently anti-capitalist slogan. He picks up the magazine, examines it more closely and gets mad all over again. He slams the magazine down on the desk, just as* PHILIP *comes into the room*) Who reads that filth around here?

PHILIP

It's Avis's, I think.

AXTON

Might have guessed it! (PHILIP *is nervous and apprehensive, holds himself tense for the next blow*) I'm sorry, Phil. Lost my temper. Fact is . . . (*A silence.* AXTON *is very self-con-*

scious, very ill-at-ease. He has to recall to himself why he came) Fact is, Philip . . .

PHILIP

Yes, Father?

AXTON

I came here for a friendly talk with you.

PHILIP

A talk?

AXTON

Yes. A friendly talk.

PHILIP

What about?

AXTON

Just—in general. How are you?

PHILIP

(*Mystified*)

I'm well, Dad. How are you?

AXTON

I'm well.

PHILIP

Aren't you working?

AXTON

Certainly I'm working! What would I be doing not working? (*This is unfortunate. It bears an implication of reflection on* PHILIP. PHILIP *so takes it. He withdraws into a shell of silence, turns away from* AXTON. AXTON *tries again*) How is everything with you?

PHILIP

About as usual. And you?

AXTON

Busy. Same old round. Always busy. Like it, though. Awful news from Europe.

PHILIP

Appalling.

AXTON

Think we'll get into it?

PHILIP

I hope not. Avis says . . .

AXTON

Don't quote Avis!

PHILIP

Sorry.

AXTON

Why does everybody quote Avis? Is Avis an oracle? Does she get her wisdom from that bolshevik rag? (*He indicates the* New Masses *on the desk.*)

PHILIP

The editor is a friend of Avis's. . . .

AXTON

Oh! Well, I hope she doesn't give them any money—her allowance money.

PHILIP

I don't know, Father.

AXTON

Well, let's not get off on Avis. Things are all right with you, aren't they?

PHILIP

Fine.

AXTON

Fine?

PHILIP

Yes, Father.

AXTON

Nothing troubling you? Nothing worrying you?

PHILIP

No. What?

AXTON

Just inquired. I'm glad. I'm glad you're happy. Life is uncertain these days. One might as well be happy. (*A silence*) I was talking about you the other day to Enid. She likes you very much.

PHILIP

(*Brightening*)

Oh, really. I'm crazy about her.

AXTON

Don't object then to my—er—you don't object?

PHILIP

I'm happy about it. I love Enid.

AXTON

I have your consent then?

PHILIP

(*Venturing a smile*)

Unconditionally.

AXTON

(*With well-meaning but in the circumstances not entirely felicitous humor*)

Give me an allowance? (*He laughs rather artificially.*)

PHILIP

Shall I give you back the one you give me, Father?

AXTON

Perhaps we'd better let things stay as they are. (*Another pause*) Well, Philip . . .

PHILIP

Yes, Father.

AXTON

I'm glad to find you well and happy. I'm glad to find you untroubled. (*He takes the plunge violently*) Because I *am* troubled!

PHILIP

(*There it is, the blow has struck—meekly*)

Yes—Father.

AXTON

In fact very troubled!

PHILIP

What about?

AXTON

About you.

PHILIP

(*He turns to* AXTON)

What have I done now, Dad?

AXTON

You've done nothing. It's I! It's I that am troubled.

PHILIP

What have you done?

AXTON

(*A grand slam of confession*)

I've neglected you—that's what I've done!

(PHILIP *blinks. This is unbelievable.*)

PHILIP

(*For want of anything better to say*)

That's all right, Father.

AXTON

It's not all right!

PHILIP

Perfectly all right.

AXTON

It isn't! Don't contradict me!

PHILIP

(*He turns away*)

Sorry.

AXTON

What I mean is—I've been in the wrong. For God's sake, Philip, stop quibbling and let's have a heart-to-heart talk!

PHILIP

All right, Dad.

(AXTON *has to regain possession of himself again.*)

AXTON

I've got to make it up to you. That's why I knocked off and came round here this afternoon. You know I don't often do that.

PHILIP

I know you don't, Dad.

AXTON

Let's start from scratch. I was, as you know, disappointed when you quit medical school.

PHILIP

I know. I couldn't help it, Father.

AXTON

I know you couldn't. Of course you'll be the first one in four generations not to follow our profession.

PHILIP

I know. I couldn't help it.

AXTON

(*Unable to keep from harping on it*)

Four generations!

PHILIP

I'm sorry.

AXTON

Once I die—for the first time in one hundred and fifty years—there'll be no Dr. Talley.

PHILIP

Maybe you can remedy that, Father . . .

AXTON

(*Puzzled*)

What?

PHILIP

Maybe you can remedy it.

AXTON

Remedy it—how remedy it . . . ?

PHILIP

Well, if you and Enid . . .

AXTON

What?

PHILIP

(*Feels it's an unlucky venture, but as he's begun it, he has to go on*)

Well, if you and Enid—I mean to say—you might—it's not inconceivable—well, I mean to say you might have a son—and he might be . . .

AXTON

(*Blushing scarlet*)

Stop it, Philip! Stop your indecorous maundering!

PHILIP

(*Almost inaudibly*)

Sorry, Father.

AXTON

(*Really angry*)

For God's sake, I give up an important patient to have a heart-to-heart talk with you and what do I get—a lot of indecorous maundering!

PHILIP

I meant—I meant . . .

AXTON

What did you mean?

PHILIP

I meant after you got married, of course.

AXTON

Stop it! Where are you going?

PHILIP

(*Turns to* AXTON)

Please, Father—please, Father, let's not have a heart-to-heart talk today.

AXTON

We will!

PHILIP

(*Yielding to the inevitable, he sits in easy chair*)

All right, Father.

AXTON

Now then—where were we?

PHILIP

I'd just interrupted the procession of Talleys.

AXTON

Don't be facetious!

PHILIP

(*Dimly*)

I'll try.

AXTON

I came here to say something to you and in spite of your very obvious opposition, I am going to say it. It is this: I was, it is true, bitterly disappointed over your failure to follow in my footsteps as a doctor. But I think that in nurturing this disappointment I have perhaps been arbitrary and narrow. I suppose there is a world outside surgery—there are other careers. I exorcise this disappointment. Let's start from scratch, Philip. Let's be friends.

PHILIP

(*Moved*)

That's most awfully decent of you, Father. Really . . .

AXTON

I want you to forgive me.

PHILIP

Oh, Dad, you make me . . .

AXTON

I mean it.

PHILIP

You make me ashamed. I couldn't have been . . .

AXTON

Nonsense!

PHILIP

Really, you do.

AXTON

Nonsense. Never mind the past. It's the future. It's the present. Let's improve those.

PHILIP

It's most awfully decent of you. Thank you, Father. Thank you very much. Don't think I didn't suffer over this. I felt all sorts of a fool and a weakling. It made me feel . . . (*He is on the verge of tears.* AXTON *is moved also.*)

AXTON

Ridiculous! My fault. Forget it.

PHILIP

Yes, Father.

AXTON

Turn your back on it. Face the future.

PHILIP

(*Looking up at him squarely and smiling*)

Yes, Father.

AXTON

(*Turns to* PHILIP)

Forgotten?

PHILIP

Yes, Father.

AXTON

Let's shake hands on it. (PHILIP *rises and they shake hands*) I feel wonderful. Don't you?

PHILIP

Marvelous.

AXTON

Marvelous sensation—to be friends with your son.

PHILIP

Ditto—with your father.

AXTON

(*He claps* PHILIP *soundly on the shoulder*)

My God, Philip—Enid's a wonderful woman!

PHILIP

Did she put you up to this?

AXTON

Not exactly. It's just her—well, you know—her influence. She's opened my eyes rather—to my own limitations.

PHILIP

(*A bit too heartily*)

That's wonderful!

(*They drop the handshake.* AXTON *lets it pass.*)

AXTON

Yes . . . Well . . . Now, my boy, the point is—to be constructive. Isn't it?

PHILIP

Yes, sir.

AXTON

Time you settled down. Why not?

PHILIP

I'd like to.

AXTON

That's what I thought. I believe in early marriages.

PHILIP

But I'm not ready to marry yet—economically.

AXTON

Well, I think we can manage that. I'm perfectly willing to help you—start you off. And when it comes to that one of these days—unless we break down altogether—Pat will be quite well off. Very well off, indeed, I should say.

PHILIP

Pat!

AXTON

Pat Ackerman. She likes you very much, I hear. (*Jocular*) Don't know exactly what she sees in you—but she sees it. I want you to know, my boy, that you have my full consent. My co-operation in every way, morally and financially.

PHILIP

But it isn't Pat I want to marry. It's Sybil.

AXTON

Sybil!

PHILIP

Yes, sir.

AXTON

Who on earth is Sybil? What kind of a name is Sybil?

PHILIP

It's not her real name. Her real name is Hannah.

AXTON

Then why on earth does she call herself Sybil?

PHILIP

For professional reasons. She's an artist.

AXTON

(*He takes a step toward* PHILIP)

An artist? What sort of artist? A painter?

PHILIP

Not exactly.

AXTON

What do you mean—not exactly? For God's sake, Philip, can't you be precise even about your sweetheart's occupation? Who is she and what is she?

PHILIP

(*In agony*)

She's a . . . She's a . . .

AXTON

My God, it must be something highly dubious.

PHILIP

(*Turns to* AXTON)

She's a dancer.

AXTON

A dancer? What sort? Ballet?

PHILIP

Not exactly. (*With dogged desperation*) In a night club.

AXTON

A night club!

PHILIP

In the Village. You can see her there.

AXTON

I'll dispense with that, thank you!

PHILIP

(*He can bear no more*)

Well, I love her and I'm going to marry her and I don't want Miss Ackerman or her money and I don't want a penny of yours, either. And some day I hope to pay you back every damned cent you've ever given me—with interest! (*He dashes out.* AXTON *finds himself alone, his appeasement policy in ruins about his feet. His anger mounts then dwindles. He considers. He came home with the best of intentions. What has happened? He feels helpless, decides to get hold of the author of his appeasement policy. He takes out a cigar and crosses to the telephone.*)

AXTON

(*Dials a number and listens a moment*)

Miss Fuller, please. . . . Thank you. . . . Hello. . . . Enid? Axton. . . . Well, I have been better. . . . I need your help. I wish you'd come over. . . . I'd rather tell you later. . . . . (AVIS *enters, puts her hat and purse on table*) How are you?

You're entertaining whom? Who's Mr. Geist? (AVIS *looks up suddenly at this*) A friend of Avis's . . . Well, here's Avis now. . . . Want to talk to her? (*To* AVIS) Here's Enid . . . Wants to talk to you. . . .

AVIS

(*In a hard voice*)

Does she? What about?

AXTON

(*Annoyed*)

Well, let her tell you. Don't keep her waiting. (*His hand is over the transmitter as he says this. He gives the receiver to* AVIS.)

AVIS

Yes . . . I'm well, thanks. . . . Is he? I didn't know you two were such buddies. . . . A publishing idea . . . well, of course, I'll be glad to talk to you about it . . . If he likes. . . . Yes, Manfred . . . I'm well, if you're interested . . . You were evidently too busy to call me today. Well, one does what one wants to do, I find. . . . Good-bye. (*She hangs up. She looks ahead of her, blind with misery.*)

AXTON

(*Watching her curiously, he sees she is under some kind of emotional stress*)

Who is this friend of yours, Geist?

AVIS

He's a friend of mine—named Geist. Or was until recently.

AXTON

What's he doing with Enid?

AVIS

Ask Enid.

AXTON

(*Looks at her puzzled; decides to drop it*)

I'm glad you came in, Avis. I wanted very much to see you. In fact, I knocked off this afternoon for that very purpose.

AVIS

Really? What for?

AXTON

Just wanted to have a cozy little—well, a nice little heart-to-heart talk, you might say.

AVIS

What about?

AXTON

Just in general.

AVIS

How?

AXTON

I beg your pardon?

AVIS

What are we going to have a heart-to-heart talk with? I mean—are we equipped for it?

AXTON

You think me heartless. Is that it?

AVIS

(*In despair*)

I wonder sometimes if I'm not.

AXTON

Nonsense. I'm sure you're very warm-hearted if you'd only let it come out.

AVIS

When are you getting married?

AXTON

Well, to tell you the truth, Avis, we've both been almost too busy to set a date. I rather wanted Enid to get acquainted with you and Philip first.

AVIS

She's doing it with a vengeance!

AXTON

What do you mean by that?

AVIS

(*Tight-lipped*)

Nothing.

AXTON

(*Irritated*)

Well, I wish you wouldn't be so cryptic.

AVIS

Sorry.

(*A moment's pause.*)

AXTON

Like Enid?

AVIS

Not much.

AXTON

(*Angry*)

Why not?

AVIS

Well, she's not my sort.

AXTON

I might have an answer to that.

AVIS

I know the answer—so much the better for her!

AXTON

What's eating at you, Avis?

AVIS

Plenty.

AXTON

Tell me.

AVIS

It would be no use.

AXTON

Try.

AVIS

You know I get on your nerves. I always have. You resent me. Why do you tempt the Fates?

AXTON

I want to change. I want to get to the bottom of the difficulty. I want to be friends with you.

AVIS

Why should you want my friendship?

AXTON

Because I love you.

AVIS

I don't believe that.

AXTON

(*Flaring*)

Well, I might if you'd let me.

AVIS

(*Clenching her fists*)

All right. I'll let you!

(*A pause.* AXTON *decides to make a mental feint before he attacks his main objective.*)

AXTON

Hear you've been in Washington.

AVIS

Yes.

AXTON

Visiting?

AVIS

Oh, no.

AXTON

Sight-seeing?

AVIS

I leave that to the tourists. I went to attend the meetings of the American Youth Congress.

AXTON

Oh, the American Youth Congress. Really?

AVIS

Yes.

AXTON

Seems to me I read about it.

AVIS

The press wasn't very fair to us. It never is.

AXTON

Weren't some of the members rude to the President? Didn't they practically picket the White House?

AVIS

What of it?

AXTON

Well, I think it's an outrage. God knows I'm not a New Dealer, but these young whippersnappers ought to learn some respect for authority.

AVIS

These young whippersnappers have so far found no authority they can respect. When they do, they'll respect it!

AXTON

It's a damned outrage.

AVIS

I could point to more serious outrages.

AXTON

You make it necessary for me to exercise self-control.

AVIS

I'm sorry. If you want to discuss things with me you must expect me to say what I think, not what I think you want to hear.

AXTON

All right, Avis. All right. I'm sorry we got off on this. As a matter of fact I wanted to talk to you about something personal. May I?

AVIS

Certainly.

AXTON

You and this fellow, Cy Blodgett . . .

AVIS

Yes?

AXTON

What sort of fellow is he?

AVIS

He's a very dear friend of mine. I like him very much.

AXTON

Is he ever serious?

AVIS

He's quite serious.

AXTON

Few times I've met him—seems to joke all the time.

AVIS

That doesn't mean he isn't serious.

AXTON

Kind of sweet on you, isn't he? (AVIS *turns away*) Like him?

AVIS

Very much.

AXTON

Well, then—why don't you get married?

AVIS

For lots of reasons.

AXTON

What's he want to be, a teacher?

AVIS

If he can get an appointment.

AXTON

Useful work. Fundamental. Now, a teacher doesn't earn much; it'll probably be difficult for you at the start. Don't let that worry you. Fortunately, I am well able to see you through your first years. I'll be glad to. If it's money holding you apart—well—forget about it.

AVIS

Thank you very much.

AXTON

Not at all. It's the least I can do.

AVIS

What makes you so generous?

AXTON

It's not generosity. You're my daughter. I feel I've been perhaps—well, unintentionally, perhaps, a bit remiss as a father and—well, I want to make up to you in any way I can.

AVIS

For what?

AXTON

(*Irritated in spite of himself*)

I'm telling you! For my limitations as a father. I feel I haven't always been completely fair to you.

AVIS

You're sure that motive isn't mixed with another—less noble?

AXTON

What do you mean?

AVIS

You're sure you don't want to marry me off so you can get me out of your way before you settle down with Miss Fuller?

AXTON

(*Aghast*)

Why, you ungrateful little . . .

AVIS

I feel no gratitude. I've never belonged to this house. You've always made me feel a stranger here. I'm not grateful to you. I don't know who I was or what my parents were. I wish you'd never transplanted me to this smug preserve of yours. I'm sure, whatever it was, it would have been better than this.

AXTON

(*Shocked*)

Avis!

AVIS

I wish you'd let me be.

(ENID *and* MANFRED *come in.*)

ENID

Hello, Axton. Hello, Avis.

AXTON

Hello.

ENID

You know Mr. Geist—Dr. Talley.

MANFRED

We have never met.

AXTON

(*In no mood for strangers, shortly*)

How do you do?

(ENID, *sensing the strain in the room, looks inquiringly from* AVIS *to* AXTON.)

ENID

Well!

(*No response from anybody.*)

AVIS

(*She turns to* ENID)

Father and I have been having a heart-to-heart talk.

ENID

(*Already not expecting too much*)

With good results, I hope? (*Her hope shattered from their*

expression) I'm afraid not. (*General silence*) Well, don't be discouraged. That sort of thing requires practice, doesn't it, Manfred?

AVIS

I dare say you keep in practice all the time. Splashing around in the milk of human kindness. Shedding sweetness and light!

ENID

Well, what would be wrong with that?

AVIS

Nothing. (*She picks up hat and purse*) Increases your circulation by leaps and bounds. And comparatively inexpensive. (*She goes out.*)

> (ENID *is confused and rather devastated.* AXTON *looks from* ENID *to* MANFRED. *He is deeply irritated.* MANFRED *affects him unpleasantly.*)

ENID

Well, really . . .

AXTON

What on earth's she driving at?

ENID

(*She turns to* MANFRED)

Manfred, you'd better go and talk some sense into her. Please go after her.

MANFRED

And then what?

ENID

You can explain.

MANFRED

Well, I'll do my best. (*He goes out after* AVIS.)

AXTON

(*Very irritated*)

Who is that fellow?

ENID

(*She puts down hat, gloves and purse*)

Manfred Geist. An Austrian refugee.

AXTON

Jew?

ENID

No. Supposing he were?

AXTON

I just asked. What are you doing with him?

ENID

I'm trying to help him.

AXTON

Help him to what?

ENID

To get established here.

AXTON

As what?

ENID

He's a brilliant writer in his own language. He's been through some devastating experiences.

AXTON

Communist?

ENID

I'm not sure exactly what his politics are. . . .

(*A moment's pause.* AXTON *is very irritated. He is angry against her, without knowing exactly what to put it on, which adds to his irritation.*)

AXTON

Avis made some strange remarks . . .

ENID

What about?

AXTON

She's impossible. I tried to get close to her. I took your advice.

ENID

Yes? What did you say to her?

AXTON

I came to her in the friendliest spirit . . .

ENID

Oh, dear!

AXTON

(*Helplessly*)

It seems I don't understand anybody!

ENID

It's the most elusive of the arts, Axton.

AXTON

I understand my own kind. That's all I want to understand.

ENID

Ah! That's a handicap!

AXTON

I came to her in the friendliest spirit . . . I talked to Philip, too. He wants to marry a dancer named Sybil!

ENID

I know. Phil brought her round to me. She's very nice. A little prudish.

AXTON

A dancer. What kind of dancer can it be that dances in a night club in the Village?

ENID

I gather her visibility is a bit high.

AXTON

Who is Philip to indulge himself with dancers?

ENID

Isn't it rather to his credit that he doesn't want to marry for money? I find it admirable.

AXTON

It's a self-indulgence. It's outrageous.

ENID

He's very young, Axton.

AXTON

At his age, I was in my second year in medicine!

ENID

Axton?

AXTON

Well . . .

ENID

I know you don't mean it, dear . . .

AXTON

You know I don't mean what . . .

ENID

You're so assured yourself. You're so masterful yourself. Don't you think you're—well, a little impatient with people who are less sure, who may be groping and uncertain . . . ?

AXTON

You seem to be on their side.

ENID

Well, I can't control a certain sympathy—instinctively I side with the underdog. What is that? An apprehension that one day conceivably one might be the underdog oneself. Nevertheless, there it is!

AXTON

What's underdog about them? They're spoiled and irresponsible. I offered to set them up! I even gave my consent to Avis to marry that learned idiot, Blodgett!

ENID

Did you?

AXTON

Well, what's wrong with that?

ENID

Do you really think it's magnanimous to dole out to people prerogatives they don't want?

AXTON

(Increasingly annoyed and hurt)

You are on their side!

ENID

No, no, no, dear, not at all. It's just . . .

AXTON

What?

ENID

It's just . . .

AXTON

Well—what is it just?

ENID

It's just that I begin to suspect that perhaps you've hidden too long in the crevices of your specialty. I am determined to lead you out!

AXTON

To what? To this rabble? Dancers and what-not! Who are all these people I suddenly find around me?

ENID

(*Simply*)

They are people, Axton.

AXTON

(*Hopelessly*)

It's a different world.

ENID

Of course it is.

AXTON

Don't understand it.

ENID

Neither do I. We have to study.

AXTON

Can't cope with it.

ENID

We must try.

AXTON

I thought you belonged to my world.

ENID

Not entirely. I don't belong to theirs either. I wish I did.

AXTON

Why, for God's sake?

ENID

You've been lucky, Axton. So have I. We found our niches early in life and stuck to them. These children find no niches. No wonder they resent us. In any case our world—the one you and I were brought up in—is done with. It's finished. And good riddance too.

AXTON

I like it. What was wrong with it?

ENID

Too many inequalities . . .

AXTON

(*After a moment he has something on his mind and feels awkward about expressing it*)

Enid . . .

ENID

Yes, dear . . .

AXTON

Avis . . .

ENID

Yes.

AXTON

She made certain dark innuendoes about you.

ENID

Did she really? Come, out with it, Axton. Tell me the worst.

AXTON

About you and that refugee fellow—what's his name?

ENID

Manfred Geist.

AXTON

About him! Mind you, Enid, I'm not cross-questioning you . . .

ENID

Darling! Dearest Axton . . .

AXTON

Only . . .

ENID

Yes.

AXTON

May I—may I just . . .

ENID

What?

AXTON

I'd like to say something to you.

ENID

Please do.

AXTON

Just once, and then forget it.

ENID

You can say anything to me. Anything at all. Come, darling—what's worrying you?

AXTON

(*He rises*)

I'll say it, just this once and then I promise you, you'll never hear a word out of me on this subject ever again.

ENID

Yes, darling?

AXTON

In your world—in your world—literary-artistic circles—Bohemian circles you might say . . .

ENID

Yes, dear?

AXTON

(*Very embarrassed*)

That sort of thing—people condone . . . Well, I suppose they don't take sexual fidelity so seriously, do they . . .

ENID

(*Soberly*)

I think they do.

AXTON

Well, I suppose there's a wide margin. Even if they're not as you might say—out-and-out promiscuous—there's a wide margin . . .

ENID

What happens in the margin?

AXTON

Well, flirtation—carrying on—you know what I mean?

ENID

Dimly.

AXTON

Well, you know, Enid, I'm awfully old-fashioned and—and —well, you might say bourgeois about that sort of thing— and I hope . . .

ENID

Yes. Tell me. What do you hope?

AXTON

(*Turns to her*)

Well, damn it all, Enid. I hope you won't make a fool of me. I hope you won't make me ridiculous . . .

ENID

Oh, my dear . . .

AXTON

You understand, I hope, what I mean, how I mean it.

ENID

I do. I think I do.

AXTON

Let's forget it then.

ENID

I do understand and I'm very touched by this, Axton. You can't possibly know to what extent—only . . .

AXTON

Yes?

ENID

I see that Avis's innuendoes—whatever they were—made quite an impression on you! I do love you, Axton.

AXTON

Sorry I mentioned it.

ENID

(*She takes his hands*)

I'm glad you mentioned it. I loved it. And let me add this, now and forever, whatever there was in the past, darling, I'm making a new life and you are the cornerstone of it. Object to being a cornerstone?

AXTON

On the heavy side.

ENID

Couldn't there be a light cornerstone? Light but durable. Duralumin. What's that? In airplanes. A flying cornerstone.

AXTON

All right, I'll be your flying cornerstone. (*He kisses her, then looks at his watch*) Oh, I must get down to the office.

ENID

Reassured?

AXTON

H'm—yes. Have to see a patient. (*She stops him.*)

ENID

Aren't you going to stay for the cocktail party? I'm giving it for you to get acquainted with your children under my auspices.

AXTON

Can't cope.

ENID

You don't have to. I will.

AXTON

All right, I'll come back . . . (*He starts to go. She holds his arm.*)

ENID

We were on the verge of a quarrel, weren't we?

AXTON

No quarrel.

ENID

(*Laughing a little*)

All right, forgive me?

AXTON

For what?

ENID

For whatever it was. (*She kisses him*) Good-bye, darling.

AXTON

'Bye. (*He goes to office door, opens it, turns to her*) Love you.

ENID

Love you. (AXTON *goes out.* ENID *is left alone.* MANFRED *comes in*) Oh, Manfred, did you patch it up with Avis?

MANFRED

On the contrary!

ENID

(*Starting out*)

Where is she? I must see her at once.

MANFRED

She's gone for a walk.

ENID

Surely, Manfred, she didn't resent my seeing you alone?

MANFRED

She did indeed.

ENID

Did you tell her I'd asked you to bring her?

MANFRED

I did.

ENID

Did you tell her it was to talk to you about some magazine commissions?

MANFRED

I did.

ENID

What a difficult child!

MANFRED

Yes, she is.

ENID

People are difficult, aren't they, Manfred? Pitiful and difficult. What was she like in Washington? You heard her speak.

MANFRED

She was very good. Passionate and convincing. You should have heard her. The whole thing was wonderful and frightening, too. I have some experience of Youth Movements. This one is coherent and articulate. But I thought of the hordes outside it, incoherent and inarticulate, the raw material of the spellbinders, exactly what Germany suffered from. I sense it on all sides—grievance without perspective.

ENID

What's going to happen, Manfred?

MANFRED

What has happened? More of the same.

ENID

Surely something will come out of all this—something better?

MANFRED

I believe so. I shan't see it. You may. Enid . . .

ENID

Yes, Manfred.

MANFRED

My daughter, Ingrid . . .

ENID

Yes, Manfred.

MANFRED

I'd like you to know her. I'd like you to be her friend.

ENID

Of course.

MANFRED

She has a rich, passionate nature. She is rather wonderful, really.

ENID

I'm sure she is.

MANFRED

Unfortunately, she is quite plain. She has never attracted men. She has turned her back then on all personal romance and has concentrated on me. Like Avis she thinks I am a great man. I would like her to meet you. I want that very much.

ENID

But certainly.

(*A pause.*)

MANFRED

I am afraid I've upset Avis very much.

ENID

How?

MANFRED

I told her finally.

ENID

What?

MANFRED

That I did not love her.

ENID

When?

MANFRED

Just now.

ENID

Poor Avis.

MANFRED

I thought I'd better.

ENID

Poor Avis.

MANFRED

She thinks it's you.

ENID

What?

MANFRED

She thinks it's on account of you.

ENID

Manfred—no!

MANFRED

It's since you came she says—that I've changed.

ENID

Manfred! How awful! How simply—! What did you say to her?

MANFRED

It didn't matter what I said.

ENID

But how utterly, fantastically . . .

MANFRED

True!

ENID

What?

MANFRED

How utterly, fantastically true! (*He laughs*) How amusing of destiny, how ingeniously sadistic, to allow me, at this moment of my career, to fall in love.

ENID

This is not fair.

MANFRED

That's what I think.

ENID

What did you tell Avis?

MANFRED

The truth—I mean—the other side of it—that I had never loved her.

ENID

You did tell her that?

MANFRED

You don't trust me suddenly?

ENID

No.

MANFRED

You may in this. Please believe me.

ENID

I must find Avis.

MANFRED

You won't in your aversion from me, forget my daughter, Ingrid?

ENID

Why do you express yourself with such violence? I feel no aversion from you. It's only that—in the circumstances . . .

MANFRED

If I had kept silence? And yet why should I not let you know that never in all my days have I met anyone so worthy of love as you? Is love so common?

ENID

It does not gain by expression.

MANFRED

In any case, where victory is impossible, what is there to lose?

ENID

There is, I think, something already lost.

MANFRED

The venture was so out of reality—as to be irresistible. To be among the homeless and suddenly to find a home. In some reserve of the mind, one still believes in miracles. It is amusing—it is very amusing.

ENID

Manfred . . .

MANFRED

Yes, Enid. Say it.

ENID

I want to say it exactly.

MANFRED

To cut off all possibility of escape?

ENID

I am deeply fond of you. I am deeply touched by you . . .

MANFRED

And yet?

ENID

There is in you something I cannot accept without reservation, something I . . .

MANFRED

Distrust?

ENID

Not exactly—deprecate . . .

MANFRED

And that is . . . ?

ENID

Some men reputed for greatness have gained in stature thereby. The reputation has stimulated the reality. You it has made cynical. The disparity amuses you merely . . .

MANFRED

Go on.

ENID

It strikes me with wonder always that with all you have suffered . . .

MANFRED

Did you think that suffering ennobles? That it filters you free of slag? No, it is happiness that ennobles. Suffering clots the soul with a fiercer desire. I know. I stand at the very outpost, my eyes on you, and I know.

ENID

The Fifth Column in every soul.

MANFRED

Yes, Enid.

ENID

There is a devastating truth in that. You seem to cherish yours, Manfred. You let it betray you.

MANFRED

Yes. One struggles against it. You could resolve that struggle for me, Enid. What suffering has failed to do—you could do.

ENID

You will have to fight it out alone, Manfred, as in the end, we all have to do.

MANFRED

There are then no miracles?

ENID

No, Manfred. Miracles are too easy.

(CY *enters.*)

CY

As I live—Miss Fuller.

ENID

Mr. Blodgett! How are you, Mr. Blodgett?

(MANFRED *rises.*)

CY

I am in the pink, Miss Fuller. In the pink.

(PHILIP *comes in.*)

PHILIP

Hello, Enid.

ENID

Hello, Phil. How are you?

CY

Hello, Manfred.

MANFRED

Hello, Cy.

CY

Oh, Phil—how's the life-class in the Village?

PHILIP

Listen here—I'm getting pretty well fed up with those bright remarks of yours!

CY

Miss Fuller—you understand child psychology. What makes Philip so truculent?

ENID

Never mind. (MARY *comes in with pitcher of cocktails, and six glasses on a tray*) Oh, there you are, Mary. Thank you. Ask Dr. Talley to come up, will you, Mary? He's in his office.

MARY

(*Horrified*)

Now?

ENID

(*Pouring cocktails*)

Well—try it. I'll take the responsibility.

CY

Yes, Mary, try it. If you don't return, we'll know you've been decapitated. Whom shall we notify?

MARY

I've got an older sister in Belfast.

ENID

Leave her name and address with the nurse . . .

(MARY *goes out.*)

PHILIP

Can I help you, Enid?

ENID

Yes, thank you, darling. Just pass those.

CY

Why don't you bring your sweetheart around, Phil?

ENID

(*Still pouring*)

I invited her this afternoon, but she couldn't come.

(PHILIP *gives a cocktail to* MANFRED.)

CY

Oh, Sybil wouldn't come to a cocktail party.

ENID

Why not?

(PHILIP *gives a cocktail to* CY.)

CY

She doesn't drink and she doesn't smoke; she just strips.

PHILIP

Shut up, Cy!

ENID

Really, Cy, you're very naughty. (*She picks up a cocktail.* AXTON *enters from office*) Here you are at last, Axton. Cocktail?

AXTON

Thank you!

(ENID *gives him the cocktail.* AVIS *enters.*)

ENID

Oh, Avis, I'm glad to see you.

AVIS

Are you? Hello, Cy—I've got good news for you!

CY

At last!

AVIS

Father is willing to set us up in light-housekeeping!

(ENID *is a bit afraid of* AVIS's *mood.*)

CY

Is this true, Doctor?

AXTON

Well, it's hardly the time or place . . .

CY

Why not? I congratulate you!

AXTON

What for?

CY

On acquiring me for a son-in-law.

AXTON

(*Intensely annoyed*)

Isn't it premature?

CY

On the contrary. Belated. We were only waiting for your consent.

ENID

(*With a look at* MANFRED, *lightly*)

Not Avis's? (*Gives a cocktail to* AVIS, *keeps one for herself.*)

AVIS

Thank you.

CY

Oh, you mean Manfred? A romantic impulse which I knew would spend itself.

AVIS

(*Bitterly*)

You're right. It has!

CY

Well! Sorry, old fellow, fortunes of war and all that sort of thing. You can't compete with youth, you know. In your heart you must have known all along that my adorable juvenility would win out.

ENID

(*Smiles at* AVIS)

What can you do with him, Avis?

CY

(*Concentrating again on* AXTON)

If I congratulate Dr. Talley it is not on acquiring a son-in-law who by the time he is fifty may well have more degrees than Nicholas Murray Butler. It is more modest than that. It is on the score of economy. Tell me, Dr. Talley, are collections slow?

AXTON

They are practically non-existent!

CY

Parallels my experience. But in acquiring me you scarcely

add to your burden. You see, Dr. Talley, essentially I'm a simple fellow. I doubt whether I shall cost you more than four duodenum a year. Maybe five—at most five!

AXTON

(*Forcing a joke*)

I shall let you have the five that don't pay.

CY

Avis, what do you mean by telling me your father has no humor?

AXTON

Did she tell you that?

CY

Why, he's delightful!

ENID

You see, Axton—the light touch works wonders!

CY

We're *en rapport*—we're beautifully *en rapport.*

AXTON

I wouldn't exaggerate!

CY

But don't let me force your hand. Shop around. I live at 116th Street and Amsterdam.

AXTON

Why do you tell me that?

CY

In case you want me suddenly.

AXTON

It is very unlikely.

CY

(*To others*)

Strong man—controls his impulses!

AXTON

When I was your age, I was doing serious work!

CY

So am I. When my Doctorate is published you will know beyond peradventure that St. Thomas Aquinas was a Marxian.

PHILIP

(*Rising*)

Well, I'm sorry, I've got to be going.

CY

Have to make the supper show?

PHILIP

None of your business.

CY

You're selfish about your girl, Philip. Awfully possessive.

ENID

Cy! Cy!

CY

He's possessive but thank Heaven Sybil isn't. She gives you her last shirt.

ENID

I don't think I love you any more, Mr. Blodgett!

CY

(*Full of commiseration*)

Don't say that, Miss Fuller! I apologize. I promise you I'll never mention Sybil again. I'll worship from afar.

PHILIP

You make me sick! (*He goes out.*)

AXTON

What kind of dancer is this Sybil?

CY

She's the poor man's Pavlova.

AXTON

How can a busy man keep up with his children?

ENID

It's a technique you must acquire.

AXTON

I thought Phil was in love with Pat Ackerman. At least, Avis, I was right about you. Or wasn't I?

CY

(*Confidently*)

You will be!

AXTON

Will be?

CY

I take the long view, Dr. Talley.

AXTON

Well, who is it now?

AVIS

Enid, you tell him! Why don't you tell him?

AXTON

(*Startled—remembers now* AVIS's *previous innuendoes*) What does Enid know about it?

ENID

Avis, why do you dislike me so?

AVIS

For many reasons.

ENID

You can't discourage me, you know. I am determined to win you over.

AVIS

Why?

ENID

Must one have a secret motive for everything? Can't it be just simple affection?

AVIS

Your graciousness is very beguiling—especially to men. But not to me. I see through it.

AXTON

(*Angrily*)

Look here, Avis . . .

ENID

Never mind, dear . . .

CY

(*Also seeing her danger, to shunt* AXTON *off*)

You mustn't be jealous, Avis. It's really Platonic between Miss Fuller and me.

AVIS

(*To* ENID)

I've been reading your poetry—the poetry, Manfred, that you admire so extravagantly. Romantic nostalgia!

MANFRED

Is that wrong, Avis?

AVIS

It's all right for those who have something to be nostalgic for.

CY

Avis, why don't you come out and have dinner with me?

I've found a new Automat. It's Aztec and it's chic. What do you say?

AVIS

I don't mind.

CY

You see. Just quivering with passion for me! Can't wait to be alone with me!

MANFRED

Why are you so hostile to Enid? She is your eloquent defender.

AVIS

(*Her head gone*)

Do you defend me, too, Manfred?

MANFRED

I explain you.

AVIS

You do discuss me then? You discuss me with *her!*

ENID

Avis, believe me, you misunderstand entirely.

AVIS

It was all right before you came. You know it was.

ENID

(*Steadily*)

I know it wasn't.

AVIS

He told you quickly, didn't he? It didn't take him long to . . .

ENID

Avis, my dear child . . .

AVIS

(*Fiercely*)

Don't patronize me! (*She turns to* MANFRED) You told her! You confide in her!

AXTON

(*To* ENID)

What is this?

ENID

I'll tell you later . . .

AVIS

Will you?

AXTON

What are you hinting? Come—out with it—what are you hinting?

AVIS

(*Ignores him, turns to* MANFRED)

Before she came, you understood me. You wanted to help me, to guide me. Now you're critical of everything I do and say. You make me feel like an immature child who . . .

(ENID *looks helplessly to* CY.)

CY

We'd better be going, Avis.

AVIS

Yes. (*She turns to* ENID) In your quiet way you're quite a man-killer, aren't you?

ENID

You'll be ashamed, Avis.

CY

Avis . . .

AVIS

Isn't Axton enough for you?

AXTON

Look here, Avis—I won't have you involving Enid in your love affairs . . .

AVIS

You're too late for that!

AXTON

Avis! I want to know what you mean by that!

ENID

Axton . . .

AXTON

I forbid Avis ever to see him again!

MANFRED

I shall gratify that wish.

AVIS

That won't be difficult for you, will it, Manfred? Thanks to her.

AXTON

You're going to come out in the open and tell me what you mean!

AVIS

As I told you before—ask Enid. (*She goes out.* MANFRED *puts his glass on mantelpiece.*)

ENID

Cy . . .

CY

Yes, Enid.

ENID

Don't leave her . . .

CY

Right.

ENID

Call me later, will you?

CY

Yes. (*He goes out.*)

ENID

Why did you say that, Manfred? About never seeing Avis again.

MANFRED

Because it is very likely to be true.

ENID

You know how much you mean to her—you shouldn't have said it.

AXTON

I'm sorry, but it seems to me that the least Mr. Geist can do is to make good that promise.

MANFRED

I shall.

ENID

Axton, you don't know the facts.

AXTON

Perhaps that is my good fortune!

ENID

Manfred is blameless in this.

MANFRED

Thank you, Enid, but that is not strictly true. As I told you—I should have disappeared.

AXTON

Well, it's not too late for that, is it?

MANFRED

(*With a smile*)

No—it is never too late for that.

ENID

Axton, when I've told you the whole truth you will regret this.

AXTON

No more than I regret it now!

(*A moment's pause.*)

ENID

Manfred—you'll bring me the magazine article tomorrow?

MANFRED

Tomorrow . . .

ENID

Manfred headed a revolution in Bavaria. He's written a fascinating article about it.

MANFRED

A memoir of failure.

AXTON

Why did it fail?

MANFRED

We were unprepared.

AXTON

Then you've no one to blame but yourselves, have you?

ENID

Axton, the world at large isn't as well organized as an operating room.

AXTON

Evidently it was, for the disciplined people who won out.

MANFRED

It was more than that—it wasn't a matter of preparation merely . . .

AXTON

What then?

MANFRED

There comes a moment in every revolution when you must kill, impartially, and by instinct. I lacked that instinct.

AXTON

Then you had no business heading the revolution. You should have stayed out of it.

ENID

I think, Axton, that without more knowledge . . .

AXTON

When you undertake a job that requires ruthlessness—you must be ruthless.

MANFRED

I am sure, Dr. Talley, that *your* timing would have been impeccable.

ENID

Good night, Manfred.

MANFRED

(*Turning to* ENID)

Good-bye, Enid. Good night, Dr. Talley.

AXTON

Good night.

(MANFRED *goes out.*)

AXTON

(*Bursts out*)

Why do you encourage that awful foreign fellow to keep seeing Avis and you? Who is he, anyway, and what's he doing hanging around you?

ENID

(*Stunned*)

That question is full of epithets. Can't you modify it?

AXTON

I feel I've stepped into a swamp.

ENID

(*Quietly*)

If you have—you have only to withdraw.

AXTON

What did Avis mean?

ENID

You are probably not aware of it but your tone—to put it mildly—is inquisitorial.

AXTON

I ask only for a simple explanation—what did Avis mean?

ENID

Are you jealous of Manfred?

AXTON

It's not my habit to be jealous.

ENID

You might be just beginning. It is only on the score of jealousy that I can even begin to explain your rudeness toward him just now.

AXTON

I wouldn't be jealous of a contemptible cad such as this fellow seems to be.

ENID

Does he?

AXTON

What else? Plays around with Avis, though he's old enough to be her father. What else is he? And where do you come in?

ENID

You shock me, Axton!

AXTON

And you do me, so we're quits rather, aren't we?

ENID

It comes back to me now . . .

AXTON

What does?

ENID

With you and Manfred before—when he came into the room with me—even before you knew any of this—your instinctive reaction was hostile. Why?

AXTON

Did you expect me to throw my arms around him?

ENID

He is a refugee. He is a sensitive man. He is an artist. He is friendless, except for us, homeless, except for us. Why was your instinctive reaction—unfriendly?

AXTON

You are demanding explanations of me *when* I want one of you.

ENID

It is because I am trying to discover between us a common speech to make my explanation—legible.

AXTON

A few simple facts are all I want.

ENID

Facts about people are often misleading.

AXTON

I'll take that chance. (*After a moment*) Is this fellow Geist in love with you?

ENID

He has said so.

AXTON

Where does Avis come in?

ENID

She's in love with Manfred, madly. Therefore—and for other instinctive reasons also—Avis hates me. She is bitterly jealous of me. Now those are the facts. How do they sound? Pretty bad, I can see that.

AXTON

You admit it!

ENID

Yes. Pretty bad—unless, as well as knowing the facts, you also know the truth.

AXTON

It all sounds very messy.

ENID

And it's very odd to me, Axton.

AXTON

Is it?

ENID

(*After a moment*)

You command an exquisite skill. You are poised and self-centered and masterful. For the practice of your profession you must have endured long years of preparation . . .

AXTON

What's all that got to do with this mess?

ENID

Simply that it's odd to me that without preparation, without study, without approach, you apply summary judgments to human beings. They are in agony—you call it a mess and let it go at that. They are homeless and friendless and in exile—they are simply awful foreigners to you and you let it go at that. You do not observe—you do not sympathize. You apply epithets.

AXTON

Well, frankly, Enid, you seem to me sloppy in your sympathies. Your sympathies are dispersed. I want them concentrated.

ENID

You want a monopoly. I can't give you that, Axton.

AXTON

(*Bursting out*)

Then I wonder why you want to marry me altogether!

ENID

(*After a moment*)

I do want to marry you. I admire and love you. But I hope, my dear, that it isn't hero-worship that you want. If you inspired that, I might burn incense at your effigy, but I shouldn't want to marry you. You are wonderfully skillful in your work. That I admire and as it saved my life, I am grateful. Really, I inhabit a world of which you know very little and that will give me privacy. Also you are strong where I am weak and that makes me want to lean on you. For all these reasons, Axton darling, I do very much want to marry you and to live with you. But don't expect me to hero-worship you. Don't expect me to yes you. That I won't do. I can't. I never will. You're too good for it, darling, and so, I hope, am I.

(*A silence.*)

AXTON

You haven't told me yet—what Avis meant?

ENID

(*It has slipped her mind*)

About what?

AXTON

About you—and this fellow Geist.

ENID

He's a distinguished man, Axton. I wish you wouldn't keep referring to him as if . . .

AXTON

And I wish, for pity's sake, you'd stop being sentimental about him because he's a refugee. If those people couldn't control a system they despise, they must take the consequences. There is a tact in conformity. As they took no interest until it was too late about what concerned them most vitally—namely, who should govern them and how—why should we now pull their chestnuts out of the fire for them?

ENID

You're a hard man, aren't you, Axton? You're a different person suddenly. Can it be that there is an obverse side to your wonderful efficiency?

AXTON

Damn it all, Enid, it's no use your treating me like a defendant in a trial, when the truth is . . .

ENID

The truth is that I am the defendant. Curious paradox in you, Axton . . .

AXTON

No paradox at all.

ENID

And yet there is Mrs. Pink . . .

AXTON

What on earth's Mrs. Pink got to do with this!

ENID

You sound like a hard man. And yet there is Mrs. Pink. Mrs. Pink who worships the ground you walk on. I don't understand. I'm bewildered. How can you be so wonderful to Mrs. Pink and to Heaven knows how many others and yet so unfeeling about this poor fellow, Manfred—your own children?

AXTON

One thing has nothing to do with the other!

ENID

Evidently not. Can it be that your kindness is exclusively professional? (*She rises*) That's an awful thought! That's a frightening thought, Axton!

AXTON

I make myself live up to certain standards—I don't coddle myself.

(*They stand looking at each other. She is seeing him as if for the first time. She is frightened and bewildered.*)

ENID

From some nameless source I feel a resentment against you. (*The telephone rings*) Resolve it, Axton, resolve it!

AXTON

(*He goes to the telephone*)

Yes . . . who . . . Just a moment, I'll see . . . Yes . . . Who wants her, please . . . ? Just a minute, please . . . (*Still holding the receiver, very irritated*) It's a Miss Geist for you!

ENID

Ingrid!

AXTON

You don't have to talk to her. I said I'd see . . .

ENID

I think I'd better . . . (*Goes to phone, takes instrument from him*) Thank you. Yes . . . this is Miss Fuller . . . Yes, Miss Geist . . . Yes, he left about a half hour ago. . . . What sort of message? Well, is that unusual? What exactly was the message . . . ? What? Hello . . . (*She clicks the receiver*) Hello . . . hello . . . (*Astonished*) She hung up on me.

AXTON

Who is she?

ENID

Manfred's daughter.

AXTON

Well, what did she want?

ENID

(*She hangs up the receiver*)

Asked me to come over right away.

AXTON

What for?

ENID

She'd just got home. She found a curious message, she says, from Manfred . . .

AXTON

What did it say?

ENID

She couldn't tell me, she said, over the telephone. I don't think she even said that. I wonder . . .

AXTON

Ignore it.

ENID

I'm afraid I've got to go. I've got a funny feeling . . .

AXTON

Call her back and ask her what she wants.

ENID

They have no telephone. She called from a pay station.

AXTON

Well, if you must go, go after dinner.

ENID

I'm going now, Axton. I've got to go now.

AXTON

What on earth for? (*Looks at watch*) It's dinner time!

ENID

Please, Axton. She wouldn't have asked me to come unless . . .

AXTON

Do you know her?

ENID

No.

AXTON

You're just crazy!

ENID

Good night, Axton.

AXTON

(*Furious*)

Well, if a call from this refugee means more to you than I do, it's well I found it out in time.

ENID

I'm sorry. I'll telephone.

AXTON

(*Shouts after her*)

You needn't. (*She is gone. He is in an uncontrollable rage. To steady himself he takes out a cigar and makes several attempts to light it*) Damn! Damn! Damn it all! Damn!

(MARY *comes in*)

MARY

Dinner is served, Doctor. Where's Miss Fuller?

AXTON

Miss Fuller has gone. And I don't want any dinner.

MARY

You look sick. Shall I send for a doctor?

AXTON

Are you being funny?

MARY

Doctors always send for other doctors.

AXTON

Well, I won't.

MARY

You look feverish. Have you got a fever?

AXTON

Mary—I have no fever. For pity's sake, leave me alone.

MARY

(*Grimly*)

You look feverish. I'll bring a thermometer. I'm going to take your temperature if it's the last thing I do. (*She turns and goes out.*)

AXTON

(*Shouting after her as she goes*)

It will be, I promise you that! (*And with all his might he flings the cigar in his hand at the door just too late to hit the vanished* MARY.)

Quick Curtain

ACT THREE

ACT THREE

At AXTON'S*—late that night.* PHILIP *is on the stage, talking on the phone.*

PHILIP

(*At the phone*)

Thanks. I'm sorry to bother you again. Be sure to tell Miss Fuller to call here when she comes in, will you? Thank you. (*He hangs up.* ENID *enters.* PHILIP *is relieved to see her*) Enid! I've been calling you and calling you . . .

ENID

I've been out. Where's Avis?

PHILIP

She hasn't been here. Does she know?

ENID

Yes. She's been at Ingrid's and gone. I wish I knew where . . .

PHILIP

Awful, isn't it?

ENID

Yes.

PHILIP

He was here this afternoon. It seems ages ago, doesn't it?

ENID

Yes. It does.

PHILIP

Talking—drinking a cocktail. What happened after I left? Anything?

ENID

(*Deciding better not to go into it*)

Nothing.

PHILIP

Nothing at all?

ENID

Nothing at all.

PHILIP

The poor daughter—did you see her?

ENID

Yes.

PHILIP

What's she like?

ENID

Very nice. Very nice indeed.

PHILIP

How did she . . . ?

ENID

She was quite calm. She was arranging things, talking to Manfred's refugee friends. There were several of them there. They were moved, but not at all hysterical. They seemed to take it for granted.

PHILIP

Gosh!

ENID

I wish Avis would come. . . .

PHILIP

Makes you think, doesn't it?

ENID

Yes, it does. (*She puts her hat and purse on the table.*)

PHILIP

Manfred—he was clever and subtle—wasn't he?

ENID

Yes. He was.

PHILIP

It's a cruel world, isn't it? People are really cruel. There is little kindness. Why is there so little kindness?

ENID

(*Thinking out loud*)

Perhaps because cruelty is at the heart of things. We won't face that. We won't admit it. Our voices are modulated and that deceives us. "We are beasts of prey," the German philosopher keeps repeating. "We are beasts of prey . . ."

PHILIP

This afternoon—when you talked to him—was there any hint . . . ?

ENID

He spoke rather strangely at the end. Some horrid idea crossed my mind . . .

PHILIP

Really?

ENID

Yes.

PHILIP

And did you . . . ?

ENID

I did nothing. I brushed it aside. If I'd faced it, I'd have had to do something about it and it was easier to brush it aside.

PHILIP

(*After a moment, trying to express the new concept of life surging in his mind*)

Enid . . .

ENID

Yes, Philip.

PHILIP

You have to be strong to live, don't you?

ENID

Yes.

PHILIP

Is Father strong?

ENID

I suppose so.

PHILIP

Why does his strength frighten me?

ENID

Perhaps because you haven't found your own.

PHILIP

I funked medical school.

ENID

Do you feel guilty about that?

PHILIP

Yes.

ENID

No reason you should. It's no law of Nature that you should be a doctor just because your father is one.

PHILIP

Enid—you really mean that?

ENID

Certainly. Find your own line and take that. There are plenty of careers still. I don't believe the world's quite exhausted yet.

PHILIP

(*He turns to her*)

Just the same I'd like to show him!

ENID

Show whom?

PHILIP

Father! I'd like to show him.

ENID

What?

PHILIP

That I can go back and stick it.

ENID

Why don't you then?

PHILIP

I believe I will. I'll go back and stick it.

ENID

Perhaps that's a good idea too. Then if you quit you'll know you've done it because you really don't like it.

PHILIP

I'll try. I'll show him!

ENID

Do!

PHILIP

If I could just know, Enid . . .

ENID

What?

PHILIP

That I can come and talk things over with you—that you'll back me.

ENID

Of course I will.

PHILIP

That's marvelous. Thanks, Enid.

(AVIS *comes in.* PHILIP *and* ENID *are both happy she has come back.*)

ENID

(*Going to her, full of pity*)

Avis!

PHILIP

(*To* AVIS, *awkwardly*)

Avis, I'm terribly sorry.

AVIS

(*Quietly*)

Thank you, Phil. May I talk to Enid?

PHILIP

Yes—of course. (*A moment*) Thank you, Enid. (*He goes out. A pause.*)

ENID

Avis, before you say anything, I want you to know—I've been thinking of you with such pain. Avis, believe me, you misunderstood.

AVIS

He left a letter for you. Here it is. (*She hands* ENID *the letter. In a strained voice as* ENID *does not open the letter, at the same time in an agony to know what it contains, his last words, his last writing*) Do you want to be alone while you read it?

ENID

No. Why? (ENID *opens the letter and reads it. It takes a second. She looks at* AVIS) Would you like to hear it?

AVIS

(*In the same strained voice*)

Don't feel you have to . . .

ENID

I want you to hear it. (*She reads*) "I didn't die today. It happened long ago. When I saw you today it was already over. I tell you this in case a shadow of reproach might cross your mind. The machine-men are stronger! To them I bow. Thank you for Ingrid. My love to Avis. Manfred." (*A pause*) Poor Manfred. He shouldn't. He should have fought on. He should have trusted . . .

AVIS

(*She turns to* ENID)

Trusted whom? Trusted what?

ENID

You. Your strength. Your love. (*A moment. She folds the letter, puts it back in the envelope. A tremendous resolution in* ENID's *face and voice*) He bowed. We will not bow!

AVIS

(*Bitterly*)

We?

ENID

Yes! We who are still free.

AVIS

Manfred is dead.

ENID

I know there are no facile consolations. But it is true, I think, that often the victims survive their murderers. (*Rather desperately*) I must cling to that belief—or I'll sink.

AVIS

It is because you did not love him that his death can be an inspiration to you.

ENID

No—but I refuse to give up. This is the moment to draw on our reserves of strength, not to yield to despair. Even Manfred was a victim. "The Fifth Column," he said, "that exists in every soul." No, I repudiate that. There are the pure in heart. There are the good. I tell you, Avis, they can move mountains.

AVIS

Why don't they then?

ENID

Because they are not together. They must find each other. They must.

AVIS

Where are they, these battalions of the good? I am sure you identify yourself with them. Where have you been all these years, you good people? I shall not forget Manfred. But neither shall I forget his murderers. It isn't alone the machine-men who murdered him. It is the rich and the comfortable everywhere who fawned on them, who admired them, who envied their efficiency. The comfortable, the complacent, the sleek! Those who didn't care who lived and who died as long as they themselves survived.

ENID

Why are you so bitter against me, Avis? Why against me who am part of you with my mind and all of you with my heart? It is as if you younger generation hate us older for having survived our errors. Resent us for having known peace and security and pleasure.

AVIS

Yes. We do.

ENID

And yet we, too, are the victims of our time. Is there any assurance that you in our place would have done better? In spite of everything you can do or say, you are indissoluble from us. We are your heirs as you are our inheritance.

AVIS

Manfred had to die at your feet. Everywhere in the world people are being slaughtered while you go on being philosophical. . . .

ENID

(*Quietly*)

It is true that our imaginations are feeble and that we do not really grieve for remote calamities. One can grieve deeply only for one person, whose voice we hear, whose step we know.

(*A moment.* AVIS *is moved. She fights it down in hard self-excoriation. She can't look at* ENID.)

AVIS

I must tell you the whole truth.

ENID

Yes?

AVIS

It isn't only that . . .

ENID

What else?

AVIS

It would be all right if I could say—my feeling against you is pure—(*She turns away*) but it isn't. It's muddied up.

ENID

Avis . . .

AVIS

I was jealous of you! I am still jealous of you!

ENID

(*Full of feeling for her*)

Avis—dearest Avis.

AVIS

It is to you he wrote his last letter. It is you he thought of at the end. I am not pure in heart. I was jealous. You are beautiful. The moment I saw you together I thought: She is beautiful. How right she is for him. I thought: I am harsh and callow. She is serene and mellow and reposeful. . . .

ENID

But, Avis, you're so wrong! I am not serene. I am uncertain and tortured and harrowed endlessly with self-distrust. I envy you your conviction, your singleness of aim—dearest Avis . . .

AVIS

You didn't love him, did you?

ENID

No.

AVIS

Why? Why didn't you love him? Enid . . .

ENID

Yes, Avis.

AVIS

I can't stay here any more with Father. I'm leaving. I've got to.

ENID

Where are you going?

AVIS

I don't know. Some room somewhere.

ENID

I can't bear to think of you going to some dismal rooming house. Why don't you come with me? I have an extra room. You can stay as long as you like.

AVIS

I couldn't do that.

ENID

I'll give you the key to my apartment. (*She takes keys out of her purse*) You can come and go as you please.

AVIS

No, Enid. I can't do that.

ENID

Why not?

AVIS

I have to think things out for myself. You have to save yourself. No one else can do it for you.

ENID

(*After a short pause*)

That's true. But don't shut me out of your life. You're good for me, Avis. (*She puts the key in her pocket*) Please think about it.

AVIS

(*She looks at* ENID *with gratitude, the gratitude of finding oneself wanted suddenly*)

All right. I will.

ENID

(*Touching* AVIS's *arm*)

Good.

AVIS

Why do you bother with me?

ENID

Because I have faith in you, Avis. Because I am as sure as I can be that . . .

(AXTON *comes in.*)

ENID

Axton—you've heard the news?

AXTON

Yes. I never really knew him. I'm sorry for you and Avis—you seem to have liked him. I ran into Mr. Blodgett. He told me.

ENID

Cy!

AXTON

Yes. I met him in the street. Avis had dismissed him, he said.

ENID

Where is Cy?

AXTON

I left him in a bar on Madison Avenue, drinking. In fact, we had a few drinks together. Not my custom! I find Mr. Blodgett more sensible tight than he is sober.

(ENID *and* AVIS *exchange a look.*)

AVIS

Father . . .

AXTON

Yes, Avis.

AVIS

I have to tell you something.

AXTON

Well . . .

AVIS

I am leaving this house, Father. I have promised myself never to sleep under this roof nor take another penny of your money as long as I live.

AXTON

As most of your allowance money goes to support filthy radical magazines I shall be glad to discontinue it.

ENID

Axton!

AVIS

No, Enid, Father is right. My presence here is dishonest. Excuse me. I'm going up to pack.

(AVIS *goes upstairs.*)

AXTON

How does a healthy man like me come to have such difficult children?

ENID

Perhaps a man has the children he deserves.

AXTON

This dispersed humanitarianism of yours is pernicious.

ENID

Not as pernicious as your concentrated selfishness. Really, Axton, it is extraordinary to me how indifferent you seem to be to the destiny of that great majority of people who don't happen to be your patients.

AXTON

Is it that I am not sufficiently grief-stricken for the late Mr. Geist?

ENID

Please, Axton, don't speak of him in that tone. I really can't bear it.

AXTON

You see, Enid, to me death is not a shock. I am used to

it. I see it daily. It is the great commonplace. I help fight it. I haven't much sympathy for those who yield to it before they have to. Why should I feel anything for an anonymous foreigner who comes into my house and makes love simultaneously to my daughter and to my fiancée? (ENID *keeps quiet. He looks at her.*)

ENID

Again you state the surface facts with no awareness of the human motives behind them.

AXTON

Well, let's drop it. I'll never say another word about it.

ENID

That's generous, Axton.

AXTON

(*With an odd, sudden look at her, quickly*)

There was something to it then?

ENID

Oh, Axton!

AXTON

(*He feels he hasn't handled it quite right*)

The truth is it's really ridiculous at my age—but the truth is I was jealous of that fellow. Plain jealous. Do you know that when you walked out on me before, I was absolutely livid with anger? I took it out on Mary. I threw a cigar at Mary. Fortunately, it wasn't lighted. Wouldn't it have been awful if I'd set Mary on fire? (AXTON *watches her narrowly, wonders if he has gained ground, goes on in the same vein*) Might have been arrested for arson. One lives and learns. Revelation to me. Didn't like myself one bit. Not one little bit. Let bygones be bygones, shall we? (*She doesn't answer*) Enid, you're not listening to me! What are you thinking? (CY *comes in. He is a changed man. His ebullience is gone. He is tight and as severely grave as an alderman. In fact he is sepulchral*) My God, he's in again!

ENID

How are you, Cy?

CY

I'm depressed. I'm very depressed. I have been sitting with Axton in the Madison Bar drinking. I looked into your very soul, Axton. A depressing vista.

AXTON

You're drunk!

CY

There is a modicum of truth in that accusation! (*To* ENID) Do you look down on me, Miss Fuller?

ENID

Certainly not. I only wish I could cheer you up. . . .

CY

I am beyond cheering up. Let's face it, Miss Fuller. I'm a failure.

ENID

Oh, come now, at your age! How do you know? You have the future. Who knows what twists and turns in the future?

AXTON

I wouldn't delude him, if I were you, Enid, with any false hopes.

CY

(*Very confidential with her*)

Supposing, for the sake of argument, Miss Fuller . . .

ENID

Yes?

CY

Supposing I do succeed in proving that St. Thomas Aquinas was a Marxian? What then?

ENID

It will demonstrate your genius for fantastic correlation.

CY

(*Anxiously*)

Are people waiting for that, do you think, in any large numbers?

ENID

I am!

CY

I shall dedicate it to you. Have you ever had a Ph.D. thesis dedicated to you, Miss Fuller?

ENID

Never. I'd be thrilled.

CY

To give you a thrill, Miss Fuller, I'd . . . I can't finish that!

ENID

It's quite all right.

CY

It was meant to build into a charming compliment—end in a graceful flourish—but I can't finish it. Can't flourish. (*The failure depresses him even more.*)

ENID

Never mind. I'll finish it for you in my own mind.

CY

She's wonderful.

AXTON

Thank you.

CY

Why do you thank me? Did I pay you a compliment?

AXTON

In a way.

CY

(*Bewildered*)

I didn't mean to pay you a compliment. I'm sorry.

AXTON

Don't mention it.

CY

I don't blame you for being in love with Enid, but why is Enid in love with you? At least I'm better off than you are.

AXTON

Now you're switching from an understandable melancholia to an unjustified optimism.

CY

(*Protesting*)

At least I don't go around saving people. He keeps saving people. For what, I'd like to know?

ENID

So they can read your historical essays.

CY

That's not his only motive. . . . (*He drifts off*) There we were, Axton and I, two jealous, frustrated men sitting in the Madison Bar. I am afraid I said too much, Axton.

AXTON

That's your habit.

CY

(*Mournfully explaining to* ENID)

The more I drink the more talkative I get. The more Axton drinks the more silenter he gets. That's incorrect. That's bad grammar.

ENID

Nevertheless I understand you!

CY

Did you hear what Sigismund, the great medieval grammarian, said when he was dying?

ENID

No. What?

CY

Just as Sig was passing out, his physician said to the recorder: "Sigismund shall die." The old boy got up on one elbow and corrected him. "You mean Sigismund will die." Is that funny?

AXTON

Uproarious.

CY

(*Sadly*)

In the Columbia Graduate School it has them in the aisles.

(PHILIP *comes in.*)

PHILIP

Enid . . .

ENID

Yes, Philip.

PHILIP

Avis is leaving.

ENID

She'll be all right. Don't worry about Avis.

PHILIP

(*Suddenly conscious that in* AXTON'S *presence he is treating* ENID *as the head of the house, to* AXTON *apologetically*)

You don't mind, Dad?

AXTON

(*Irritatedly*)

Mind what?

PHILIP

Well, I mean—my asking Enid . . . It's only that I . . .

AXTON

I wish you wouldn't be so vague, Philip!

CY

I sympathize with you, Axton. You are a frustrated man.

AXTON

I wish you'd shut up!

CY

I know a good psychiatrist. Or maybe if you just came up and talked to *me* every day. I'm not a natural listener, but I could try.

AXTON

(*In despair*)

Enid, will you shut him up?

ENID

Shut up, Cy.

CY

Do you really mean that, Miss Fuller?

ENID

Yes. I do.

CY

I shall enter a Trappist monastery and take a vow of silence.

(AVIS *comes in, wearing hat and coat, putting on gloves*)

AVIS

Hello, Cy.

CY

Hello.

PHILIP

Please, Avis, don't go.

AVIS

I have to.

PHILIP

I'll be lonely.

AXTON

When she's here you fight like cats and dogs.

PHILIP

I'll miss it.

AVIS

Would do you good to leave, too, Phil. Might make a man of you.

AXTON

You see, Enid, what can I do? She's impossible!

AVIS

Good night, Phil.

PHILIP

Good night, Avis.

AVIS

We won't lose sight of each other.

PHILIP

Please not.

AVIS

Good night, Enid.

ENID

Here's the key, Avis. You go ahead.

AVIS

(*Takes the key*)

Thank you. Good-bye, Father.

AXTON

Good-bye.

AVIS

Coming, Cy? (*She goes out.*)

CY

There is no balm in Gilead. What do you suppose that was,

Axton, that balm? Can you write me a prescription for it? Maybe we can still get some on Madison Avenue.

ENID

You'd better go home as soon as you can and get some rest.

CY

Rest for what? Quoth the Raven: Nevermore. The Raven said it. Where are the snows of yesteryear? God, I am not a man. I am an anthology! (*He goes out. A moment's silence.*)

PHILIP

Do you think she'll come back?

AXTON

My guess is she'll be back in a month.

PHILIP

What do you think, Enid?

ENID

I don't think so.

PHILIP

What'll become of her?

ENID

She's tough.

PHILIP

I wish I were tough.

AXTON

(*Brusquely—can't bear to have* PHILIP *think himself inferior to* AVIS)

You're all right, Philip!

PHILIP

No, I'm not.

AXTON

You're all right. I wouldn't have you like that intractable, unfeminine little wisp of a Spartan for anything in the world. You're all right, I tell you.

PHILIP

I wish I hadn't fought with her. Half the time when I fought with her, something said to me: She's right and you're wrong!

AXTON

It's the other way round. What's the matter with you, Phil? Haven't you got any spirit at all?

ENID

Axton! Please!

AXTON

I only want him to stand on his own feet.

ENID

He will. Don't worry about that. He will!

PHILIP

(*To* ENID)

Have you told him—about my decision?

ENID

No. Not yet. I will.

PHILIP

Please do. Good night, Dad.

AXTON

Good night, Phil. Don't worry about anything. You're all right.

PHILIP

(*Defiant*)

I will be! Good night, Enid.

ENID

Good night, darling. (*She goes to him rather unpremeditatively, and kisses him.* PHILIP *is so overcome by this tenderness that he is about to burst into tears. He rushes out before it happens. There is a pause.*)

AXTON

What did he mean—Phil? What decision was he talking about?

ENID

He feels a sense of guilt evidently—about medical school. He thinks perhaps he ought to try again.

AXTON

(*Delighted*)

Really? (*Exultant*) That's wonderful. Marvelous. He's a doctor, Enid. You'll see. Every Talley's a doctor. I owe you for this. Thank you, Enid.

ENID

I wonder why it is . . .

AXTON

You wonder why what is . . .

ENID

Why it is so often that the sons of strong, successful men are beaten at the start?

AXTON

Phil's not beaten. You'll see. I'll keep him under my eye. He'll come out of it. I'm sure of it.

ENID

He's frightened. He's a frightened boy.

AXTON

Nonsense. He hasn't hit his stride yet, that's all. He'll hit it now. He's all right now, I'm sure.

ENID

Axton . . .

AXTON

Yes, Enid . . .

ENID

Doesn't it strike you as strange that within fifteen minutes of meeting your children I learned more about their personal lives than you seem to have discovered in as many years.

AXTON

Well, children will talk to the policeman on the corner before they'll talk to their parents. Don't you know that? I was the same way.

ENID

Why don't you face the truth, Axton.

AXTON

What truth?

ENID

That you are a failure as a father. I am very much afraid that the Talley Method isn't enough. It seems to be wonderful on anaesthetized tissue. For human beings not yet anaesthetized, I'm afraid it's a little bit arbitrary.

AXTON

(*Cajolingly*)

It worked with you!

ENID

Oh, my dear, if your approach in the operating theater were as fumbling as it is in your living room I shouldn't be here to tell it. Nobody would.

AXTON

Well, in spite of my clumsy approach, Phil's coming

through. I can't tell you, Enid, how pleased I am about that. And grateful to you. From now on things should go smoothly. (*Whistles energetically with relief*) Bad moment or two. Well, thank heaven it's over. We've survived our first quarrel. (ENID *looks at him quickly*) Well, not exactly quarrel—let's say misunderstanding. May there never be another! Enid, what's the matter? What are you thinking?

ENID

The truth is—I feel sick at heart.

AXTON

Why?

ENID

That I should have been so wrong.

AXTON

What about?

ENID

About you. About myself.

AXTON

Perhaps we're not as far off as you think.

ENID

We're world's away.

AXTON

With improved communications we might get in touch.

ENID

Don't humor me, Axton.

AXTON

My God, Enid, have I been wrong about you? Are you capricious?

ENID

I don't really think so.

AXTON

What do you mean then, for God's sake, by talking like this? Just when everything's getting settled.

ENID

No, it isn't. Everything isn't settled. It's far from settled. It's very unsettled.

AXTON

For instance.

ENID

I suppose that in ordinary times you and I might have made a go of it. But these are not ordinary times.

AXTON

What have the times got to do with this?

ENID

Everything. You can no longer live in a sound-proof room —in a spiritual autarchy.

AXTON

I thought you were making a new life—that I was to be its cornerstone.

ENID

That was before I found out—before I saw . . .

AXTON

What?

ENID

Your effect on those around you. I have come to see—reluctantly—I have come to see that your effect on those whom you cannot aid with your mechanical skill is destructive. You are arrogant, Axton. You want to impose your ideas and your way of life on others. You have no more sense of the individual than a machine-gun.

AXTON

Who are you to pass these judgments on me?

ENID

It's what I think. I have seen you with your own children.

AXTON

I must tell you, Enid, that I think your sympathy for the children is maudlin. It's what's ruined them—a whole generation of them.

ENID

Come now, you can't condemn an entire generation.

AXTON

Each generation has to justify itself. My father went on with his researches while he saw his fingers burned off with radium—his hands reduced to stumps. Yet he got less for it than these young revolutionaries on the dole, which they find insufficient. Don't talk to me about these impromptu hordes in this country or any other. I despise them and the cant that caters to them.

ENID

You have a contempt for people, Axton.

AXTON

The truth is—you're a sentimentalist. I'm a realist, that's all.

ENID

The realists seem to have a wonderful capacity for turning their backs on injustice and suffering.

AXTON

It's that I can't endure muddle. Don't you see that? I love order. I watch the disintegration of the cell and I feel a cold fury inside of me that I cannot stop it.

ENID

What about the disintegration around you? Why doesn't that arouse you to fury—a fury against yourself? Since coming into your house I have seen wretchedness, Axton. I have seen suffering. I have seen blundering. I have blundered also—had I spoken differently to Manfred—had I found the word—a word that might have saved him. I didn't find it. I didn't say it. I have been clumsy and inadequate also. But you shut your failure away from you. You are consoled because you save people's lives. But you have to do more than save people's lives. You have to give them something to live for. No, Axton —there is a realm beyond efficiency. Through you I became gay again and strong again and confident again . . .

AXTON

Well then?

ENID

But you don't really want me that way. You prefer me as I was. You don't want a companion to share with you and differ from you. You want a patient. Well, I am cured now. I am strong now. I am myself now. I want to use the life you gave me freely and abundantly. I don't want to hoard it. You live in a vacuum into which you want to draw me. I'm frightened, Axton . . .

AXTON

(*He takes a step toward her*)

What are you frightened of, for God's sake?

ENID

There are destructive forces in the world now of violence and ruthlessness, and I am frightened of the things I find in you which are like those forces. I'm sorry, Axton, but I can't possibly marry you.

AXTON

(*Deeply shocked*)

You're leaving me . . .

ENID

I have to.

AXTON

My God, you're not going to let a difference in point of view separate us.

ENID

But that's all that ever does separate people. In the passion of first love—in youth—such a difference might be obliterated. But you and I . . .

AXTON

What good does it do me to be right if I'm miserable?

ENID

Forgive me, Axton, but that seems to me so unscientific. There must be something wrong or you wouldn't be miserable. Isn't pain a symptom?

AXTON

I am willing to make concessions.

ENID

I don't want concessions. I want a change of heart, Axton. Can you perform *that* major operation?

AXTON

It isn't exactly fair to make me pay for not living up to your romantic idealization of me.

ENID

Perhaps not. It must have been your professional manner.

You warned me against it. But it's so beautiful, Axton, you can't blame me for being taken in by it. Better modify it in the future or you'll get involved again.

AXTON

Don't talk rot. It's either you or nobody, and you know it damn well!

ENID

That's very sweet of you . . . (*She puts on her hat and picks up her purse.*)

AXTON

(*Gloomily*)

It'd better be nobody, I guess. I can't cope.

ENID

Maybe you could . . .

AXTON

It's too late.

ENID

Nonsense. In a sense I'm going to begin again . . . (AXTON *looks at her sharply*) with your children, for instance. Avis is at my house now. I'm going to keep her with me for as long as I can.

AXTON

You're a masochist.

ENID

No, on the contrary—I've got two new interests. It'll be great fun. I'm really grateful to you, Axton. I've always wanted to have children. Thank you very much.

AXTON

I don't like you! Definitely!

ENID

I keep telling you. Good night, Axton. (*She goes to him and offers her hand. They shake hands.*)

AXTON

Shall I take you home?

ENID

No, you're tired. You have to operate in the morning. I want to walk anyway.

AXTON

Then it's hopeless?

ENID

For the good-willing, it's never quite hopeless. Why don't you try it, Axton?

AXTON

What?

ENID

The major operation.

(*A second's pause. He starts toward her, appeal in his eyes, in his voice.*)

AXTON

Enid . . .

ENID

(Unwilling to have her emotion for him stirred up again at this moment. She has been through enough for one day)

Good night, AXTON.

(A moment longer—their eyes meet. She turns and goes out, a little blindly. He takes a step after her, her name on his lips.)

AXTON

(Though she is gone, to himself)

Enid . . . Enid . . .

(But she is gone. He is alone. He stands, rooted, thinking. How has this happened to him? He feels himself suddenly spent, nerveless. He is overcome by a feeling of despair and, what is more unexpected for him, fear, a fear of loneliness, a fear of the future, that he has never felt before. This devastates him. He sinks into a chair, trying to seize this fear, to wrestle with it, to overcome it. He cannot. He feels it overcoming him. He stares at the floor, his fists clench. . . . The curtain comes down.)